P9-CRO-606

Homesteads

Homesteads

Early buildings and families from Kingston to Toronto

Margaret McBurney and Mary Byers

Photographs by Hugh Robertson

UNIVERSITY OF TORONTO PRESS

Toronto Buffalo London

© University of Toronto Press 1979
Toronto Buffalo London
Printed in Canada

Publication of this book has been assisted by grants from the
Laidlaw Foundation, the Ontario Arts Council, and the Canada Council.

Canadian Cataloguing in Publication Data

McBurney, Margaret, 1931-

Homesteads

Bibliography: p.
Includes index.
ISBN 0-8020-2357-6

1. Historic buildings – Ontario. 2. Pioneers –
Ontario. 3. Ontario – History – 1791-1841.*
4. Dwellings – Ontario. I. Byers, Mary, 1933-
II. Title.

FC3062.M22   971.3'5'02   C79-094583-5
F1057.8.M22

Frontis: 219 Keith Street, Whitby, the Robert Wilson House

CONTENTS

MAPS

On the following pages are a general map of the region and detail maps of the area covered by this book.

Throughout the book, buildings in urban areas are normally identified by street addresses, and in larger centres local maps may be needed to find them. In rural areas buildings are generally located by concession and lot number. The location of some houses is not given at the owners' request.

The townships of Upper Canada were surveyed in concessions separated by 'concession lines,' usually one and a quarter miles apart. The concessions themselves were divided into lots, each of which had two hundred acres.

In most townships, the concessions are simply numbered, with no other designation. In Prince Edward County, however, some concessions have names which refer to geographical points of land, e.g., concession 1 southwest of Green Point or southeast of Carrying Place. The designation Broken Front refers to the lakeside concession which, cut by bays and inlets, does not have unbroken frontage.

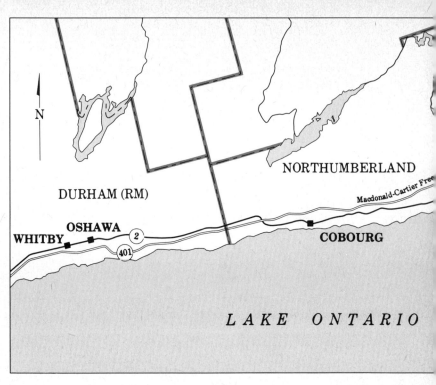

N

DURHAM (RM)

NORTHUMBERLAND

Macdonald-Cartier Free

OSHAWA

WHITBY 2

COBOURG

401

LAKE ONTARIO

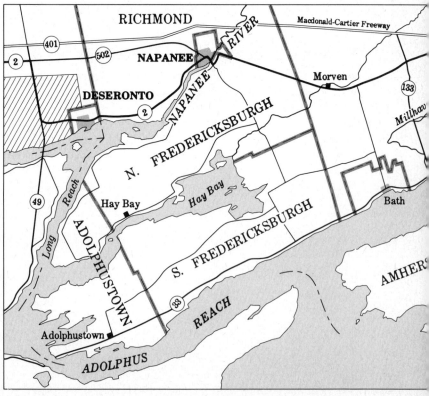

RICHMOND

Macdonald-Cartier Freeway

401

NAPANEE

502

2

Morven

DESERONTO

NAPANEE RIVER

133

2

Millhav

N. FREDERICKSBURGH

49

Hay Bay

Hay Bay

Bath

Long Reach

ADOLPHUSTOWN

S. FREDERICKSBURGH

AMHERS

33

REACH

Adolphustown

ADOLPHUS

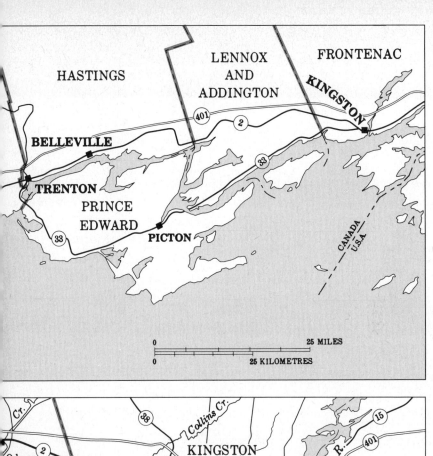

HASTINGS

LENNOX
AND
ADDINGTON

FRONTENAC

KINGSTON

401 · 2

BELLEVILLE

TRENTON

PRINCE
EDWARD

33

33

PICTON

CANADA
U.S.A.

0   25 MILES
0   25 KILOMETRES

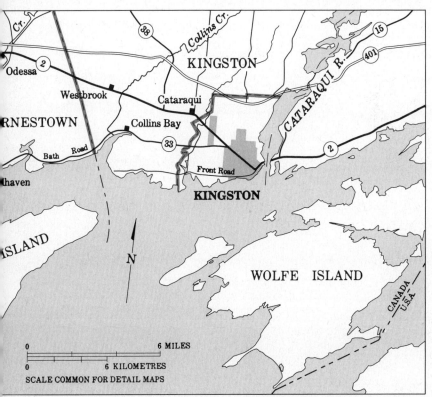

Cr.

38

Collins Cr.

15

401

2

Odessa

KINGSTON

CATARAQUI R.

Westbrook

Cataraqui

RNESTOWN

Collins Bay

2

Bath   Road

33

haven

Front Road

KINGSTON

ISLAND

N

WOLFE   ISLAND

CANADA
U.S.A.

0   6 MILES
0   6 KILOMETRES
SCALE COMMON FOR DETAIL MAPS

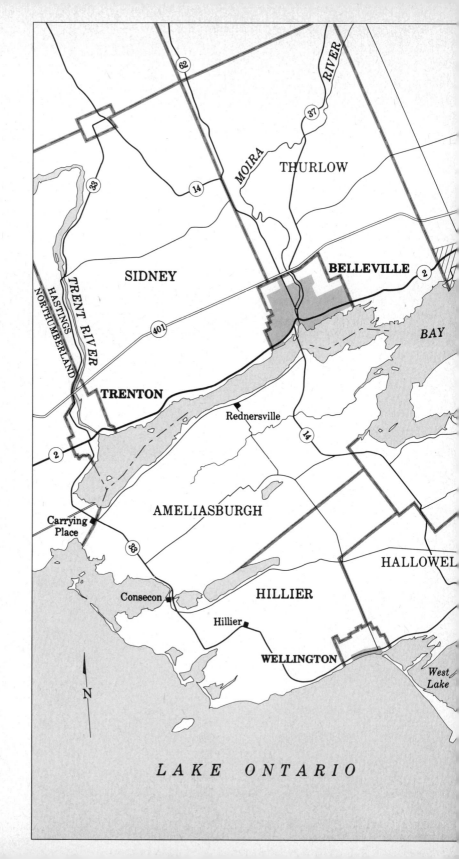

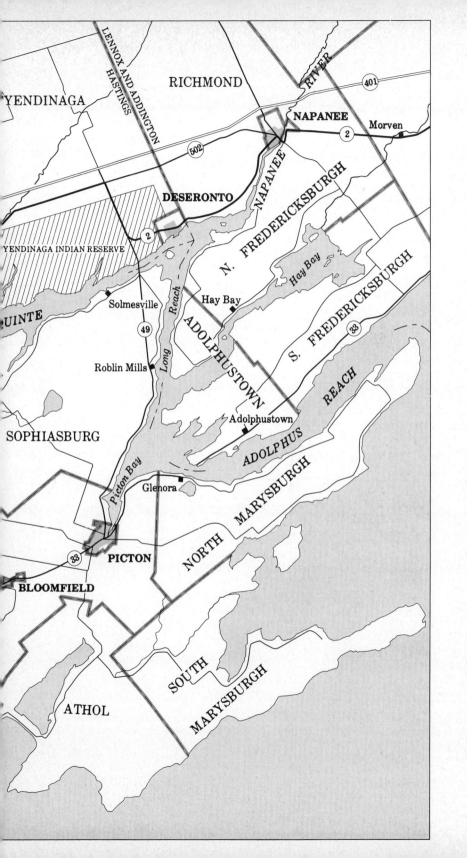

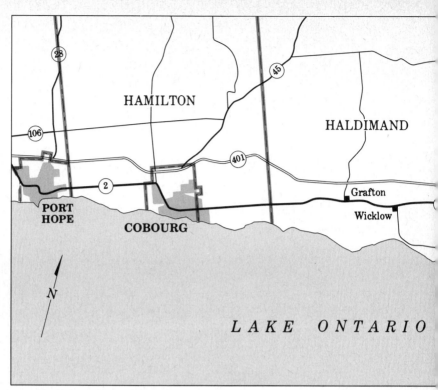

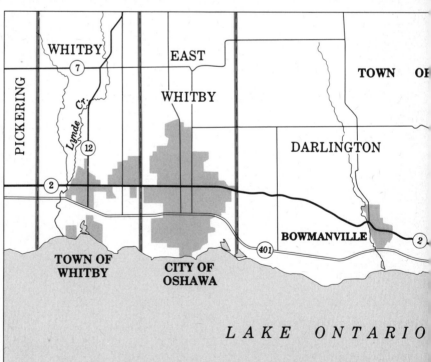

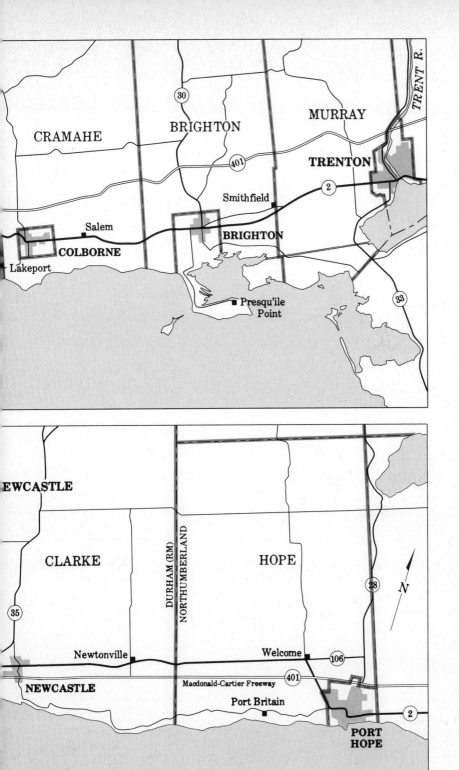

William S. Goulding (1917-1972)

We wish to acknowledge a debt of gratitude to the late William S. Goulding, whom we knew as Professor of Architecture at the University of Toronto. His work in stimulating and then supervising a province-wide inventory of pre-Confederation buildings in Ontario was, itself, a formidable piece of pioneering. The records that have resulted are invaluable, and the volunteers who assisted in the survey (of whom we are but two) have continued to support the cause of historic preservation in their communities.

At the time of his death, Professor Goulding was working on a book about Ontario's early buildings and the society in which they were erected. The Ontario Ministry of Culture and Recreation had made a grant to the University of Toronto Press to assist in the publication of that projected book. That grant the government has kindly re-allocated to this volume. We hope that it will help to foster an interest in and an appreciation of Ontario's architectural and social history – a cause to which Bill Goulding made such a lasting contribution.

Homesteads

INTRODUCTION

The first 'roads' in Upper Canada were the waterways. Although Indian trails existed along the shore of Lake Ontario, its waters provided the pioneer with dependable and more comfortable access to vital mills and equally vital neighbours for much of the year. In winter the frozen lake also formed a passable route. Before the turn of the nineteenth century, nevertheless, Asa Danforth, an American surveyor, was at work widening the trails to form the colony's first official road. His job was made slightly easier in parts by the fact that the first settlers had opened some stretches of primitive roadway already.

Danforth's commission was part of Lieutenant-Governor John Graves Simcoe's larger plan to build a military road, to be called the Dundas Road, traversing the province from Detroit to the border with Lower Canada. Danforth was responsible for the section from York to Kingston. His orders, signed in 1799, were to provide a route which was 'smooth and even' and to build bridges in such a way that all 'precipices, steeps and sudden descents ... shall be made safe, gradual and easy.' Once completed, the road was to be maintained by statute labour, that is by the local landowners who were required to work on the roads a certain number of hours each year. It was difficult, if not impossible, to cut a road through the wilderness which would be 'smooth and even' with slopes both 'gradual and easy.' But even where that could be achieved, the victory could be short-lived. Only in the townships just west of Cataraqui were settlers located in sufficient numbers to perform statute labour and keep the frontage clear. Where settlement was sparse, nature took over soon after Danforth had cleared the path, and gradually filled it in.

In spite of all difficulties, Danforth completed his work in three years. His first road still exists in some places, such as the section between Port Hope and Newcastle.

During and after the threatening years of the War of 1812, the government decided to cut a York-Kingston road further inland, less vulnerable to attack from the lake. As a result the Kingston Road was completed between 1816 and 1817. Much of its path lay in the first and second concessions, up from the shore. At the same time, it incorporated some sections of the Danforth Road which were the most direct link between established settlements.

The Danforth and then the Kingston Road served settlers on their journeys on foot, on horseback and by stagecoach until the railroad provided another means of travel in the second half of the century. The present Highway 2, called 'Heritage Highway,' still follows some sections of the Danforth, but takes a distinctly different path for about half of its length. It does not include the old road which stretched from Kingston to Adolphustown and through Prince Edward County from Glenora to Carrying Place.

In writing this book, we set out to investigate the living history connected with the pre-Confederation buildings along these three early roads – the Danforth, the Kingston, and Highway 2.

We wish to emphasize one point. The buildings included here are only a selection from the many of similar age still standing. In making the choice, we have tried to give a feeling for the unique history of each community along the route. We could not include everything. A book could be, and in some cases has been, written about each locale. Our guidelines for selection were the following: the building should be on or near one of the early roads; it should be of pre-Confederation date; it should have architectural interest either as a 'pure' example of a style or a local adaptation. Inevitably, however, our interest began to focus on the people who built or lived in the houses: they built much more than the structures of wood, stone, and brick. Having made our own rules we felt free to bend them when a building seemed too important to pass by. In Cobourg we included the houses built by 'the Americans' which, although of later date, were an integral part of the town's life in the nineteenth century. We fervently hope that our choice will whet the reader's appetite for the lively history of the nineteenth century as represented in the buildings of the time. If time permits a detour from the speedways, the effort will be rewarded.

The dating of buildings is full of pitfalls. Local legend tends gently to push back the date as time goes on. In some cases, yearly assessment rolls exist which neatly categorize dwellings into 'round logs, squared timbers, frame, brick or stone of one or two storeys.' When such definitive material is lacking, financial assessment rolls, newspaper articles, diaries or some such original documents are useful. Much of this material is preserved for study, in the original or on microfilm, in the Ontario Archives in Toronto. Beyond this guesses can be made on the basis of architectural style or mortgage records, but we have resorted to this type of dating only when all else failed and have pointed out when it occurs. After all, architectural styles did not suddenly end in a particular year, especially in remote areas, and may have continued long after a new style had emerged elsewhere. And mortgages on a property do not necessarily indicate that money was borrowed to build a house; they can also mean that funds were needed for other purposes.

Local legend, a relatively minor factor in dating buildings, looms much larger in the stories we discovered of life along the road. Marvellous tales abound concerning buried treasures which, it seems, were concealed all along the route. These stories most often concern a pay load which was hidden by an agile driver when robbers were in pursuit. Sometimes, though, the treasure went down in a ship in the lake, or was hastily hidden by a company of militia and never found again. From time to time a dig is organized but no great cache has ever been publicly announced. Legends of tunnels located along the lake are also frequent. These tunnels were purported to be escape routes from various forms of attack or handy things to have in days of Prohibition. Such legends and more are part of a verbal history handed down over the years and later recorded. Embellishments have frequently crept in over two hundred years, but it is difficult not to feel that there may be some truth at the core. For the purposes of accuracy, however, we have noted when legend is part of our story. The only truly reliable sources lie in original documents of the time – census records, assessment rolls, diaries, wills, land titles, etc.

As our acknowledgements indicate, we have spent considerable time pursuing such original sources in the Ontario Archives and in communities along the route from Kingston to Toronto. We are also greatly indebted to the local historians who preceded us. Their works are listed in the select bibliography at the end of this volume. The earliest of them, and the one we have had occasion to quote most often, was Dr William Canniff, author of *A History of the Early Settlement of Upper Canada*, which was published in 1869. Dr Canniff was then thirty-nine years old. He had been born in Thurlow, studied medicine at Toronto, and practised in that city and Belleville. He also did what many of us today may wish we had done. He talked to his grandparents and to everyone's grandparents still living in the Quinte area – and he wrote it all down. In some cases he was able to talk directly with men and women who had come to Upper Canada with the Loyalists as young children. He thus gave us an invaluable record of the early settlers, from people who experienced the immigration or had heard about it from parents who had lived through it.

One difficulty which we encountered in studying the settlement of the late eighteenth and early nineteenth centuries was in the spelling of surnames. The only certainty is that there was constant variation. A single example is the Herkimer family who cleared land near Kingston. The descendants of Johan Jost Herkimer also spelled their names Herchmer (as on the Crown grant issued to Nicholas Herkimer for Herkimer's Nose), Herchimer, and Herchimere. We have attempted to use an early spelling of each family's name, as found on some legal document, knowing however that there is no single 'correct' spelling to which we could turn.

A myth we learned to set aside is that of the 'good old days' which depicts the pioneer period as one in which the work ethic prevailed absolutely, idleness was non-existent, and life was simple although rough. Professor Northrop Frye has said of such myths of past innocence: 'Pastoral myths are mostly illusions projected from the experience of growing older ... A child's world seems simple and innocent to an adult ... But however natural it may be it is clearly nonsense; there never have been any simple ages.' By the mid-nineteenth century, newspapers were already commenting on the death of the first settlers and referring to them as representatives of a stock the likes of which would never be seen again. In 1800 life was very hard but not very simple. It does an injustice to the age to romanticize it.

The subject of the Loyalists we found fascinating. The term Loyalist was used in the Revolutionary War as a synonym for American colonial Tories who sided with the British. The terms United Empire Loyalist or Loyalist have since then been used generally to denote those American colonists who preferred British rule and took refuge in Canada after the war. The official use began in 1789, when Lord Dorchester, the governor-general, passed an order-in-council in Quebec directing that those who had been loyal to the Crown and had suffered in the Revolutionary War and were now in Canada should be registered in government documents as UE, the term indicating the great Loyalist principle of Unity of Empire. The term UE subsequently was used by governments of Upper Canada and Canada West in land registries to mark those Loyalists and their children who received special land and government privileges. Today, the United Empire Loyalist Association of Canada brings together the descendants of UEL families and helps those who wish to discover if they qualify for the affix UE.

In the early 1800s, Loyalists were often either saints or sinners, depending on whether the writer was British or American. Descriptions of one type left the impression that without exception they had blood of royal blue in their veins and acted solely out of love of the Crown. At the other extreme the Loyalists were seen as traitors who, lacking any feeling for their country, left for Canada to get cheap land. The truth probably lay between these poles. Certainly the majority who deserved the affix UE came to Canada to live under a British form of government and lost homes and possessions in the process. Without question, too, there was much persecution in the American colonies of those who would not support the Revolution. Loyalists were tarred and feathered. Many were hanged and many who came to Canada had seen their neighbours hanged. There were some however who, having failed to support the rebels without being actively Loyalist, lost their livelihood in the United States and came to Canada for economic reasons. No doubt some also came for the cheap land and for no loftier motive. Many family splits developed over the question of loyalty to the Crown or to the revolution – tragedies that more often than not resulted in separations which were never mended.

When the Loyalists came north in the 1780s they brought their remaining possessions with them – and counted among their moveables were slaves. There was a heavy concentration in Loyalist country of slaves, many of whom had fought for the Crown in the Revolutionary War and would fight again in the War of 1812. Many of the families who appear in this book had slaves as part of their household – the Van Alstines, Meyerses, Herkimers, Cartwrights, Bleeckers, Cronks, Laziers, Finkles, and others. Slaves were frequently sold. One of them was Henry Finkle's Mary, described in the deed of sale as 'a female Negro slave ... about five feet five inches high and twenty-five years of age.' Her price was £25 and her purchaser, Joseph Allen, by the deed had rights to 'have, hold, occupy, possess and enjoy the said hereby Granted and Bargained female Negro Slave Mary.'

Perhaps it is not widely known that Canada led the fight to end slavery. As early as 1792, in the first Legislative Assembly held in Upper Canada, Lieutenant-Governor Simcoe proposed that slavery be abolished. Since many of the members of that Assembly were slave owners, in particular members of the Executive Council, the proposal was not enthusiastically received. Simcoe did however secure a law that no more slaves could be brought into the country, and that all children of slaves already in the country would be freed on reaching the age of twenty-five. This step was taken forty-one years before Great Britain abolished slavery.

Much could be said about the role of women in the 1800s. Since pictures speak louder than words, the situation even late in the century is best stated in a series of illustrated county atlases published in 1878. Drawings romantically depict men's houses, their well-tended fields, and those dearest to their hearts: their horses, sheep, and cows, usually with a mention of their names. Rarely is a wife to be seen. She was in fact another possession, as indicated by the numerous newspaper notices which proclaimed that a certain wife had left her husband's bed and board with absolutely no provocation and no person was to harbour her or give her credit.

The lady of the pre-Confederation house was usually made of stern stuff. She did heavy manual labour while producing a child nearly every year, many of whom never lived to maturity. Dogged determination must have been a feature of her make-up, as epitomized in one lady of the Herkimer family. Convinced in her heart that no child born on Canadian soil could be truly a British subject, she insisted upon travelling to Great Britain each time she became pregnant. On each trip she took her favourite chairs in case she should become ill and never return to Canada. She was the mother of eleven Herkimer babies, a feat which entailed twenty-two ocean voyages.

Nineteenth-century newspapers contained an amazingly detailed coverage of world events, but some small local items give the flavour of the times more clearly. Advertisements make good reading. T.J. Jones, dental surgeon, advertised in the *Bowmanville Statesman* in 1868 that his 'Improved rubber teeth bore away the prize at the Provincial Exhibition in Toronto.' A fellow dental surgeon offered to perform extractions with or without pain, the choice being up to the patient.

A further comment on that simpler, sweeter age are the stories that held the widest popular appeal, judging by the frequency with which they appeared. They contained a goodly amount of violence, as in this item from the Hallowell *Free Press*, 25 June 1833:

On the last trip of the Canadian Eagle to Quebec, when the engineer, Mr James Laing, went down below to oil the engine, his foot slipped, and on falling back the spoke of the fly wheel struck him on the head and instantaneously killed him. His body was dragged in by the wheel in its revolution, the limbs torn off, the body torn into fragments, and although he was naturally a corpulent man, so minutely were his remains ground that they passed, we are told, through a hole not more than sixteen inches in diameter!

Wills are valuable research tools not only as inventories of a person's holdings but also as reliable sources of genealogy. They also have priceless human interest. One resident of Ernestown, in dividing his earthly possessions, stated that 'Horace and Frank is to divide my clothes up between them – most of them will come good for mops if nothing else.' The same gentleman left sufficient to his wife 'to keep her chewing.'

If our research has been a pleasure and a privilege it also has a serious goal – to increase awareness of the historical importance of our early buildings. Many dedicated citizens are at work now to ensure that no more of the best of their local architecture is lost. It is evident when a community has an active historical society, for the results of their efforts are readily apparent in a drive through the area.

A fitting conclusion to two years of research occurred during our final visit to the owner of a home we have included. While sitting in the log house watching the same churning lake which greeted the Loyalists, we were introduced to his two dogs. Their names put the finishing touch to our work – George Brown and John A.

1

The Bath Road

The Bath Road that starts the journey west from Kingston, through Collins Bay to Adolphustown, is a heritage highway in the fullest sense. On it Asa Danforth lived, at Finkle's Tavern near Bath, while he was building the first official road through the bush for ninety dollars per mile. The road follows the shore of Lake Ontario, in an area that saw naval skirmishes during the War of 1812 and on whose streams were built the first mills in Upper Canada. It is the route, as well, that the Loyalists took before there were roads, when they came in 1784 to settle in the townships west of Cataraqui. Its name recalls a time when Bath was a noted shipbuilding village and the site in 1816 of the launching of the *Frontenac* – the first Canadian steamer to navigate Lake Ontario.

The road (the present Highway 33) meanders through the first four townships to which Sir Frederick Haldimand, as governor, directed those who had served the Crown during the American Revolution. The townships of the St Lawrence River and the Bay of Quinte were named for members of the royal family of George III and have been referred to as the Royal townships although those west of Cataraqui were more commonly known as the Cataraqui townships. The first was called Kingston, in honour of George III himself. To it came a company of Loyalists, civilians from New York, under Captain Michael Grass. Westward along the road the second township, Ernestown, was named for Prince Ernest Augustus, Duke of Cumberland and later King of Hanover, the eighth child of the king. It was settled by American Loyalist veterans who had served with the British under Major Edward Jessup. Further west, the third township, Fredericksburgh, was named for Prince Augustus Frederick, Duke of Sussex, the ninth royal child. It was settled by soldiers who had served in Sir John Johnson's Regiment, Major John Ross's King's Royal Regiment of New York, and Major James Rogers' King's Rangers. Westward again, the fourth township, Adolphustown, was named for Prince Adolphus, Duke of Cambridge, the next royal son. Into it came a party of Loyalists, civilians from New York, under Captain Peter Van Alstine. The Bath Road ends at Adolphustown where the Glenora Ferry crosses the Front Bay to the shore of Prince Edward County. From Kingston to Adolphustown, every single lot was taken up in the 1784 settlement. This is United Empire Loyalist country.

Near the western limits of Kingston, south of the Front Road at 86 Sunnyacres Road, a simple stone building overlooks the lake. It was built by the shore for a practical reason, for water pre-dated the Front Road as a means of travel. Peter Wartman, a Loyalist, built the house in 1803, according to family tradition supported by local research.

Peter's father, Abraham Wartman, and his mother, Christiana Wessenberg, had been in Captain Grass's party. Christiana, reputed to have come from a titled family in Bohemia, had eloped with Abraham when she was twenty and journeyed with him to New York. The Wartmans remained loyal to the British Crown and came to Canada in 1784. From generation to generation through the Wartman family it has been said that when Abraham first sailed along the shore of this unsettled wilderness he saw a large rock projecting into the lake. He said to Peter, 'That stone marks the land I want.' Michael Grass agreed to the request.

Abraham lived for only three years after he arrived. By the time that the Crown patent was issued in 1802, it was in the name of Peter, who was living in a log cabin on the property. The rock that prompted the land selection can still be seen a few hundred feet east of the Wartman house. Names of early members of the family are carved on its surface.

Young Peter Wartman married Captain Grass's daughter, Eve. They had twelve children and were luckier than many parents of the time: nine of the youngsters survived infancy. The small house they built by the shore of rough limestone, a storey and a half with a gabled roof, is typical in its symmetry. The house has changed little over the years. Its original locks and bolts remain on the panelled doors; the cupboards, chair rails, hardware, and floors are all unaltered. Peter lived to the age of fifty-nine. His wife survived him by thirty-four years. His descendants treasure his commission papers in the Frontenac County militia, appointing him an ensign in 1799, a lieutenant ten years later, and a captain in 1821.

At the southeast corner of the Bath Road and Day's Road (484 Day's Road) is the house built by Calvin Day, for whom the road was named. In the early 1800s, when few families had settled and travel was difficult, inter-marriages between neighbouring families were frequent. Two members of the Wartman family married into the Day family of Kingston. Peter Wartman's brother, Barnabus, married Hannah Day and Sarah, his daughter, married Calvin Day. Hannah and Calvin were descendants of Barnabus Day, who had accompanied Michael Grass on an initial survey of the settlement area in 1783, and remained at Cataraqui to continue the work.

Peter Wartman house, 86 Sunnyacres Road, south of the Front Road

The two-storey limestone house, with its central peaked gable, was built by Calvin in the 1850s. The property previously was owned by Robert Miller, who took out four mortgages, amounting to £815, during the 1830s; it is thus possible that Miller had built a dwelling which Calvin enlarged or replaced after purchasing the land in 1849. With him, Sarah lived in a much more substantial home than the simple cottage down the road in which she had spent her youth. The difference is evident in the stone itself – finely cut and worked in contrast with the rough stone of the earlier dwelling.

'Herkimer's Nose' was the local name for a point of land at the west end of the Front Road (lot 1 and the gore, concession 1, Kingston). It was named after Nicholas Herkimer, who farmed his land there with his wife Charlotte Purdy. The Herkimers had been at home in the wilderness areas of America for over a century before moving to Upper Canada. Johan Jost Herkimer, Nicholas's grandfather, had traded with the Indians in the Mohawk Valley in the early 1700s. When the Revolutionary War began, the family divided. Captain Johan Jost, son and namesake of the fur trader, sided with the Crown, was imprisoned, and later escaped to Niagara and then to Cataraqui. Nicholas Herkimer, the fur trader's other son, became a general on the American side and lost his life fighting against the king.

Two of the Loyalist's sons cleared land in the wilderness of Lake Ontario – Nicholas at Herkimer's Nose and his brother Lawrence at Smith's Creek, later Port Hope. Lawrence had established a thriving business trading in furs and was living in a log house when the land on which he had settled was granted by the Crown to Jonathan Walton. Lawrence was unable to prove he had bought the land legally from another trader. Enraged but undaunted, he moved to Cataraqui and became a successful merchant. Nicholas secured a Crown grant to the land at Herkimer's Nose in 1803 but was murdered six years later. His widow and family remained at the family homestead, holding the land until 1834. In later years Nicholas's brother Jacob caused a local stir by winning the hand of Margaret Hickman England, a lady who had been the object of the attentions of John Strachan and to whom the future bishop wrote romantic poetry. The 'understanding' between Margaret and Strachan was terminated by her marriage in 1803 to Herkimer, who already had several children by a Chippewa wife. After Jacob Herkimer's death, Margaret married twice, the second time to a clergyman in Bishop Strachan's diocese.

The Herkimer land was purchased in 1834 by Robert Drummond of Kingston, a shipbuilder and distiller who died of cholera that same year. In 1836 the property was sold once more and tragedy continued. The buyer, William Lemoine, a retired British army captain, died soon after the purchase, and his son froze to death following an accident which occurred when he was returning from Collins Bay alone one night. In 1864, a fire destroyed the Herkimer-Lemoine house. The home of Kingston limestone the Lemoines then built (now numbered 2000 Front Road) can be seen from the nearby public park.

The peace that prevails there today is in sharp contrast to an event during the War of 1812 described in *A History of the Early Settlement of Upper Canada* by Doctor William Canniff: 'About five miles from Kingston lies what is called Herkimer's Point. It was thought a thing not improbable that the Americans might land upon

Lemoine house, at the end of the Front Road

this point and endeavour to enter Kingston ... At last, one morning, the Yankee fleet composed of some 14 sail, large and small, appeared off the Upper Gap ... the fleet passed along not far from the shore, and field artillery moved along at an equal pace and firing kept up between them.' The enemy did not land at Kingston but proceeded down the St. Lawrence.

The original Bath Road did not take a straight path through Collins Bay as it now does but curved north through the Moses Smith property (lot 3, concession 2, Kingston). Moses Smith purchased the site in 1812 but it is uncertain whether he built on it. His wife, Hannah, was the daughter of a Loyalist, George Buck, who had served as a guide for the Crown in New York State, despite being crippled, and made the journey to Upper Canada. The Smith family held the land at the foot of Collins Bay for nearly ninety years, the longest tenure being that of Samuel Henry Smith who built the house now standing on the property shortly after the deed passed to him in 1837. The gabled end of the limestone building has a fine door with side and transom lights. This helps to date the house: the practice of putting the main door in the gable end became popular about 1840. Some original glass is still in the windows. The redirection of the Bath Road has given the Smith homestead a quiet location at 1693 Hillview Road.

Captain Daniel McGuin, a merchant from New York, arrived with Michael Grass and took land west of the Smith property on Collins Bay. With Daniel came his son Anthony, who built some of the first mills in the area. Initially Anthony built a carding and fulling mill, then later a grist mill, both on Collins Creek. He was a young man in a hard country, and it was probably due to lack of experience that he erred in locating his grist mill: in any case, the water in the millpond backed up and flooded his neighbours' lands. The neighbours sued young McGuin for £300 and won their case. This was an enormous sum at the time, and it must have staggered the young miller.

But McGuin settled the debt and went on to build a saw mill. He eventually became a prosperous and influential man. In 1806 he married Mary Morey. Their family grew to five sons and four daughters. By 1832 the McGuins were able to build a stone house (lot 1, concession 2, Kingston), set well back from the Bath Road overlooking the lake. Sadly, Mary McGuin died of consumption before they moved in. The house, Loyalist Lodge, was originally a one-storey Georgian structure with a central doorway flanked by large windows. It has been much altered over the years by a series of additions, but these must not have been made until the latter half of the century, for the 1851 census still listed Anthony as living in a single-storey building. It describes him as a yeoman and miller, aged seventy-eight.

McGuin died two years later. He left large parcels of land to each of his six children still living and to his son-in-law, Hugh Rankin, the widower of his deceased daughter Mary. It would appear that McGuin knew his children well, for the last paragraph of his will states: 'I also will that in the division of my personal property among my heirs as before mentioned, my son John shall NOT have any share of the money as he has a propensity to squander whatever he gets, but an equal share of all other personal property.'

A short distance to the west is the home of Anthony McGuin, Jr. After his father's death, Anthony purchased the grist mill from the estate. The younger McGuin was well established by this time and had already begun construction on his own house at 4111 Bath Road. The work was completed in 1854 with the help of a mortgage for £1,750. Two years later, disaster struck. A fire completely destroyed the mill. With the help of other family members, Anthony rebuilt it within the year.

Anthony McGuin never married. He was a successful businessman who was known to all as the 'governor.' His pleasant house was originally a simple limestone structure to which a small addition was made in the late 1860s – possibly to provide living quarters for his housekeeper. The stone cottage and carriage house to the east of the building were added a few years later as were the dormers and the large verandah which conceals much of the façade.

Along the Front, at 4097 Bath Road, is the David John Rankin house. In 1849 news of a gold strike in California quickly travelled as far as Upper Canada and, as elsewhere, many young men were tempted to go west. David John, a grandson of the elder Anthony McGuin, caught the 'gold fever' but was persuaded by his uncle, Anthony Jr, to stay in Collins Bay and help with the family mills. By the early 1860s he had become general manager. Possibly in recognition of his work, his childless uncle built a house for him in 1862. A compact stone building of two storeys, it stands between his uncle's and grandfather's homes. The addition of a wing on the west side of the house a few years after its construction softened the austere lines. Later, some of the small-paned windows at the front were replaced with larger panes of the 'modern' variety, but otherwise the exterior remains as it was.

Not far to the west of the Rankin and McGuin houses is a handsome stone building set well back on a broad expanse of lawn. 4255 Bath Road was built by Peter C. Aiken. Little is known of the Aiken family apart from a few clues gleaned from census records and assessment rolls. From these sources it appears that Peter arrived in Upper Canada in the early 1820s with his parents, Robert and Martha Aiken. Seven more children were born to the family, and the census of 1851 shows them all living in a single-storey frame house. Three years later, Robert Aiken bought fifty acres of land, but he died the month after the purchase. In 1862, Peter took out a mortgage, presumably to build a house on the property inherited from his father. The house is of grey stone; its front door, with side and transom lights, is flanked by single windows at either side. The

David John Rankin house, 4097 Bath Road, Collins Bay

dormers are a later addition. There were no fireplaces in the house when it was built and for almost a century it was heated only by stoves. Not until 1948 was it provided with a furnace and electricity.

Westward, in Ernestown, is the Samuel D. Purdy house (4403 Bath Road). Samuel was a member of a prolific family which settled in the area after the Revolutionary War. His grandfather, Gilbert Purdy, had been a guide in the British army. After Gilbert's death in 1788, several of his children and possibly his wife left their home in New Burgh, New York, and came to Upper Canada.

The oldest in the family of eight was David. He received as a grant from the Crown the east half of lot 41, concession 1, Ernestown. Four years before that, however, he had purchased lot 42, immediately to the east, from Rev. John Stuart. The house which stands on the lot today was probably built by his son, Samuel D. Purdy, shortly after 1860 – at any rate, a mortgage was taken out at that time. With its panelled door and balanced lights, peaked

Samuel D. Purdy house, 4403 Bath Road

gable and rounded window, it is a superb example of proportion and symmetry using simple materials. The builder's uncle, also named Samuel, started the first stage line in the area. It went from Kingston to Bath in 1816 and the next year was extended to York. The fare was $18.

One of the first Loyalists to arrive in Ernestown was Joshua Booth, who had been a sergeant in the Revolutionary War. Booth built one of the earliest mills in the township at Millhaven. His Crown grant, which is dated 1803, was several miles to the east however, on lot 41, concession 1, west half, Ernestown. Booth later built other mills and became a large landholder. In 1792 he was elected a member of the first Legislative Assembly and served for four years.

The Booth house at 4423 Bath Road near Amherstview, was built before 1813, but presumably replaced an even earlier dwelling on the lot. It had two storeys with spacious rooms to accommodate

Stonewatch, home of the Booth family, 4423 Bath Road

Joshua's wife, Margaret Fraser, and their ten children. Across the road lies Lake Ontario. The Booths called their home Stonewatch because, according to legend, it was built during the War of 1812 and served as a lookout for approaching American ships. Joshua died suddenly in 1813, aged fifty-four after only a short time in Stonewatch, leaving his property to his son Benjamin, also a miller. Benjamin had married Catherine Dorland in 1809 and by the time of his father's death had located at Mill Creek, now Odessa, and built mills of his own. He therefore deeded this property to his brother, Charles A. Booth, and it remained in the latter's hands until 1873. It is believed locally that the house was at one time a coach stop.

Years ago the bodies of two sailors were washed up on the lakeshore across from the Booth house. A story is told that the men were buried on the property, and that one of them haunts the house. Members of the present family and their guests have heard heavy footsteps pacing the upper hall or slowly climbing the stairs. One evening, when the present owner was preparing tea, she felt a shove in her back. When she turned, she found that she was alone in the room. Determined to pursue the mystery, she waited one night until she heard footsteps on the stairs. Racing to the head of the staircase she turned on her flashlight; the steps continued but nothing could be seen. The owners claim that they do not believe in ghosts and yet no other explanation is forthcoming.

The Fairfield White House, just west along the road (lot 37, concession 1, Ernestown), dates from 1793. Solidly anchored in limestone bedrock, its frame walls are strengthened with brick and stone fill. The bricks were fired in kilns on the property, the timber planed at an Ernestown sawmill built in 1789. Other building materials were ordered from Richard Cartwright in Kingston.

William Fairchild and his son Archibald had served in Jessup's Corps in the Revolutionary War and came to Upper Canada with Jessup, along with William's wife, Abigail, and six other children. The family grew to include six sons and six daughters. When they first arrrived on their land, the Fairfields like other new settlers erected a temporary log building. They made plans immediately for the present frame house, to which was later added a two-storey verandah. The Fairfield children and four slaves assisted in the construction. Their only heat for almost twenty years was from fireplaces, until stoves became available around 1812.

The White House exemplifes the Georgian style which was popular among Loyalist settlers. A Georgian house could range in size from a single storey to two storeys with an attic, as in this instance, and could be built in frame, stone, or brick. Its hallmarks were symmetry (as in the placement of the windows), balance, and proportion. Both inside and outside there was a sense of hospitality, epitomized in the entrance and the main hall. The front door of the White House is given extra 'presence' by the addition of four panes of glass on either side of it and the transom light above.

In 1805, William Fairfield deeded the east half of lot 37, on which the house stood, to his son Stephen – 150 acres with the Broken Front (the irregular lakeside portion of the land). At this point Stephen already had an innkeeper's licence, and a tavern probably operated in part of the large house during the rest of his tenure. At his death, William left all the land west of the house to another son, John, and his wife, Elizabeth Clapp, on condition that 'the said John Fairfield shall support my affectionate wife and aged mother during their life times.' Apart from that, he left to each of his sons only ten shillings because they were already established; the remainder of his substantial holdings he gave to his six daughters.

A daily swim in the Bay of Quinte during the winter might not have universal appeal, but it was the habit of one of the first residents of the village of Bath, Rev. John Langhorn, who would 'cut a hole in the ice, and another at some distance, and would dive down at one hole and come up at the other.' This and other singular habits of Mr Langhorn are recounted in Dr Canniff's *A History of the Early Settlement of Upper Canada*. Langhorn travelled, founded Anglican parishes, and performed marriages for twenty-six years. The marriage records he kept are important historical documents today. His parishioners found however, often to their dismay, that he would not officiate at a wedding unless it was held in a church and before noon 'no matter how far they had come, generally on foot, or by canoe. Sometimes they were from remote townships, yet they were sent away unmarried.' He was Welsh, a man of strong opinions, high morals, eccentric habits, and great girth. Langhorn conducted a dedicated ministry, travelling routinely as far as Carrying Place. 'Being somewhat corpulent, he never rode. His plan was to sling his surplice and necessary outfit, including a Bible and Book of Common Prayer for service, in a knapsack on his back and so set forth on foot to visit his scattered flocks.' When he left to return to Great Britain in 1813, the Kingston *Gazette* remarked that many who knew him 'would have reason to recollect him with gratitude and to regret his removal from the country.'

While he lived in Bath, Langhorn occupied the western part of a small log house built by Jeptha Hawley in 1785. The site, on the Bath Road west of the town, is marked by a provincial historical plaque, but the house has been so altered that it bears little resemblance to the original log building.

In 1796, when Langhorn was still in Bath, a frame building was completed which still stands at the corner of Main and Church Streets. It was called Fairfield Place and was owned by the Fairfield brothers, William and Benjamin, sons of William, Sr, the pioneer of the White House. The brothers became successful and prominent men and played an active part in the life of the growing village. They were both, at different times, members of the Legislative Assembly of Upper Canada. The property had been deeded to

Home of William Fairfield, Bath Road, completed in 1793

William by the Crown in 1801 but Benjamin lived there, and on William's death in 1816 it was left to him. William had his own residence and what must have been a thriving business, for the inventory of his effects taken at the time of his death contained more than the average family's needs, including 26 gallons of wine, 21 gallons of brandy, 80½ gallons of spirits, 39½ pounds of tea, 17 spelling books, and 16 cross-cut saws.

Since then Fairfield Place has undergone many changes. The gable and dormers on the south side are later additions, as is the wing on the east side and a small porch with rooms above it on the north. Changes have been made to the interior as well. The house remained in the family until the 1860s. For many years afterwards it was a fishing lodge called Bay View Villa, and then, in 1938, it was bought by one of Benjamin's descendants. On her death it became the property of the St Lawrence Parks Commission with the following dedication: 'This house of peace and pioneer memories was given to the Province of Ontario as a thank offering for this haven of refuge provided for my United Empire Loyalist ancestors who left their homes and all their possessions in the colonies to seek sanctuary under the British flag.'

The steamship industry in Upper Canada was founded in Bath. It was financed by a group of leading citizens, including Henry Finkle, the tavern owner, and his wife – a lady with the memorable name of Lucretia Bleecker Finkle. The first steamboat built there was the *Frontenac*. Its cost exceeded £20,000 and on the day of her launching in 1816, Dr Canniff recorded, 'the boat moved slowly from her place, and descended with majestic sweep into her proper element.' In the early part of the nineteenth century, Bath was a busy community rivalling Kingston as a business centre. Shipping and shipbuilding were its main industries but it also boasted carriage-makers, iron foundries, saddleries, tinsmiths, and various other artisans.

Bath also has the beautiful and weathered Davy home, built in 1819. Along with the Fairfields and the Finkles, the Davys were prominent in the commercial life of the village. John Davy of Little Falls, New York, arrived in 1784 and three years later married Sophia Hoffnagel. She bore him eight children and, several years after his death, married John Walden Meyers of Belleville (Meyers' Creek). John Davy's Crown grant consisted of all of lot 10 in the first concession of Ernestown. In his will he bequeathed this and other parcels of land to his sons and divided his other goods and chattels among Sophia and his daughters.

John and Sophia's eldest son, Peter, was a farmer, shipbuilder, merchant, and tavern keeper. In 1819 Peter built a handsome house, neo-classic in style, on the north side of Academy Street. Here he and his wife Aurelia Chapman raised twelve children. Now the house stands empty and desolate. At one time it was undoubtedly the finest in the village.

Peter's brother, Benjamin Fairfield Davy, began his business life as a storekeeper. Other brothers, George and William, worked with him. In 1838, Benjamin started a new venture in Napanee, leaving William minding the Bath store. From Napanee, Benjamin moved to Whitby and later again to Belleville where he became the first mayor of that city. William Davy remained in Bath and some time during the 1840s built the W.H. Davy store at the corner of Main and Davy Streets. This fine building, recently restored, is one of two

Davy Store, Main and Davy Streets, Bath

limestone buildings in the village. It was planned both as a residence and a store, the door on the west end leading to the commercial area. Most of the building's original windows remain. Of particular interest is the main door which is nearly a replica of the door on the Peter Davy house, although the latter was built more than twenty years earlier.

William Davy also built a small house at the north end of the village. It is a modest cottage, much altered now by the addition of a verandah across the front. Records suggest that the house was built after the store but this seems surprising as the living quarters in the store were far more elegant.

Another Davy house remains in the village, built by Peter R. Davy. A small storey-and-a-half building, it was designed for two families and originally had two doors on the north side. The house is on the south side of Academy Street, east of Lodge.

During the early 1800s Bath's Main Street was lined with commercial buildings, each with a two-storey verandah facing the road. Sadly, all but one were destroyed by two disastrous fires. The one remaining, on the north side east of First Street, was built by E.D. Priest in the 1820s. It is now deserted and in poor condition but it does help one imagine how the once-busy street used to look.

Bath never fulfilled the promise seen for it by the Fairfields and Davys. The village was bypassed, first by the York Road (Highway 2) and later by the railroad. The declining fortunes of the shipbuilding industry also played a large part in undermining the economic health of Bath and other communities along the bay.

In contrast to the business activity, Bath's spiritual well-being flourished in the mid-nineteenth century. Anglicans, Methodists, and Catholics were all actively involved in building or expanding their respective churches.

Anglicans worshipped in St. John's, a small church built by the first settlers in 1793. It served them for more than a century until it was destroyed by fire in 1925.

A few blocks to the west, on Academy Street, the Methodists built a small, spartan structure in 1849; only the later addition of a tower provided it with some architectural interest. Money was scarce and not to be wasted on frills in the 1840s. The Methodists had worked hard to raise the funds necessary for even so modest a church, and for years afterward the congregation held tea-meetings

Methodist Church, now United Church, Academy Street, Bath

to liquidate the mortgage. As well, the Ladies Aid Society held yearly bazaars and 'in three years raised $250.00 to expend in improving the exterior of the Church.' In reporting this the *Christian Guardian* added, 'It is really wonderful how much may be accomplished by the rapid movements of the tiny fingers of that sex, whose taste is always graceful and refined.' The original narrow clapboard was stuccoed over in 1955.

About halfway between the Anglican and Methodist (now United) churches, south of Academy on Davy Street, is an interesting board and batten building which was used for many years by the Presbyterians. It was not, however, designed as a church but as a hall for the local Mechanics' Institute. Such institutes, patterned on British models, spread rapidly in Ontario during the nineteenth century. They provided education for working men, through lectures and library facilities supported by membership fees. There were nearly three hundred in the province in 1895, when by legislation they were converted into a free library system covering the province.

The members of the Bath Mechanics' Institute ran into trouble, however. When their new hall was completed in 1859 they were unable to pay the bill presented by the carpenter, Abraham Harris. As a result, Harris found himself the owner of the ornate frame building. He immediately rented the lower hall to the Presbyterian Church and the upper to the Masons. According to a recent study by members of Queen's University, Harris subsequently built up a debt with his physician which he could not pay, and on his death the church became the property of Dr Roderick Kennedy. The doctor transferred ownership to the Anglican Church with the proviso that the Presbyterians retain the main floor. This they did until after church union, when they moved out and left the whole building to the Anglicans. They in turn eventually sold it to the Women's Institute.

Today the 'layercake church' – as it came to be known when different congregations worshipped on its two floors – stands neglected, its future uncertain. Yet it retains a certain raffish charm. It is a handsome example of the gothic revival in board and batten, with its large gothic window and flowing bargeboard. The three-arched arcade, behind which the front doors shelter, testifies to Harris's skill.

When the residents of Bath decided to build a town hall in 1861, a

The 'layercake church,' originally the Mechanics'
Institute, Davy Street, Bath

Town Hall, Main Street, Bath

classical revival style was chosen. This fitted with the general belief of the times that civic buildings should reflect the dignity and respect for democratic ideals considered inherent in classical architecture. The small frame town hall on the north side of Main Street, west of First Street, served for many years as a court house. It was also used for town meetings, auctions, and even badminton games. With its four-columned portico, it is Bath's only classical revival building.

One of the early residents on the Bath Road to the west of the village was Conrad Huffman, a former member of the King's Rangers. His Crown grant for lot 1, concession 1, Ernestown, is dated 1798. Conrad first built a log cabin, but some time after 1812 he began construction on a two-storey home which still stands solidly by the bay. He made the bricks for it at the back of the farm, and must have spent considerable time hand-planing all the interior woodwork, doors, and baseboard trim and the solid wooden shutters

Conrad Huffman house, lot 1, concession 1, Ernestown, just west of Bath

which helped keep in heat. Heavy pegged beams and hand-made nails can still be seen. Four of the six fireplaces have panelled side cupboards which held china and utensils to keep them warm.

In 1833, following Conrad's death, the property passed to his eldest son, Adam. Since Adam had established himself in a home nearby, he sold the house and land to his brother, Conrad Jr, for £100. Conrad Jr may already have been living in his father's house. He had married Jane Shibley in 1804, a union which produced twelve children. Jane's parents, John and Ellen Shibley, had settled just west of Bath at what became known as Finkle's Point, site of the shipbuilding enterprise. Family legend has it that as they approached the site, the enthusiastic young Ellen jumped from the boat in which they were travelling, grabbed an axe, swung it at a tree, and declared, 'Now I have cut the first tree on our farm!' This is the stock that Ontario's settlers sprang from.

The westernmost of the Cataraqui townships, Adolphustown, was settled by a party who arrived by boat in 1784, at the end of a journey which had brought them from New York the previous year. Among the group who followed Captain Peter Van Alstine was one Daniel Cole. Family legend maintained that he had been sentenced to hang as a spy by the rebels but had literally slipped out of the noose around his neck, evaded the rebels' bullets, and made his way to New York and finally to Upper Canada. He settled in Adolphustown and lived to be one hundred and five years of age. At his death, according to Dr Canniff, he left eight children, seventy-five grandchildren, one hundred and seventy-two great-grandchildren, and thirteen great-great grandchildren. The single-storey white frame house on lot 11, concession 1, Fredericksburgh Additional, stands on land purchased by Henry Cole in 1833. Since this property is on the doorstep of Adolphustown it seems not unreasonable to assume or hope that Henry must be one of Daniel's descendants. The same year that he bought the land, Henry took out a mortgage, suggesting that he could have started building at once. Interior details attest to the present house's age. Subsequent owners have changed and enlarged the building, but have not effaced its original simple lines and fine design.

Adolphustown was the first settlement west of Cataraqui. Samuel Holland, surveyor-general of Canada, sent a party under John Collins to the site of the village in 1783, to prepare for the coming of the Loyalists. The Bay of Quinte was then a wilderness. The settlement was first called Hollandville, and from it parties laid out the lots in the Bay of Quinte townships that the Loyalists took up in June 1784. For the next four years, the site was used as a centre from which the government rations (a pound of flour and a pound of beef or pork daily per adult and a half ration per child) were distributed. These supplies continued until the Loyalists were able to raise enough in their clearings to feed themselves. Today Adolphustown is the focus of Loyalist attention on the Bay of Quinte. The old Allison house is a Loyalist Museum. The Loyalist cemetery stands by the shore. The frame parish hall of St Alban's Church was built in 1822–3. It was originally a church in its own right – St Paul's – and served as such until St Alban's was built to commemorate the centenary of the Loyalist landing in 1784. The Adolphustown township hall, built by 1840 in frame, was part of an early court house.

The cradle of Methodism in Upper Canada can be reached by a short detour just east of Adolphustown. Few eighteenth-century

Henry Cole house, lot 11, concession 1, Fredericksburg Additional, east of Adolphustown

buildings are still standing in Ontario and of these only a handful are of frame construction, one of the least durable of building materials. The Hay Bay church (lot 18, concession 3, Adolphustown) represents in itself the best of pioneer construction. In its history it holds the story of the persecution of the Methodists and the financial sacrifices of the first settlers.

Before Rev. William Losee, the first officially appointed Methodist preacher west of the Maritmes, took over the Kingston circuit in 1791, two Methodists, a teacher and a preacher, had been expelled for acting in opposition to the established Church of England. By 1792, however, Losee had gathered a congregation large enough to merit a church. The land was given by Paul Huff, one of the Disbanded Troops and Loyalists listed in 1784. The building was financed by its congregation. Gifts ranged from £1 to £15, the latter sizeable subscription coming from Conrad Vandusen who, according to *The History of Methodism in Canada*, had been a tavern keeper until, influenced by Losee's preaching, he took an axe to his tavern signs.

The old church stands by the bay, a sight even more soul-stirring from the water than from the land, for this is the way it was seen by its parishioners as they came to worship. The lack of passable roads, and the need therefore to use the lake for transportation, were the chief considerations in the selection of the site. Its beauty was a natural by-product.

The original church was a two-storey building, rectangular in shape, with a central doorway in the middle of the long axis. A window above the door and two on either side produced a pleasing symmetry. The church seemed a part of its surroundings and proved what could be accomplished, even in those early days, by carpenters who had mastered their trade and followed their intuitive sense of proportion. In 1835 renovations became necessary and the church was enlarged by one third. This necessitated some changes in the basic structure.

Over the years the building served as a court house and also, during the War of 1812, as a barracks. For John A. Macdonald, the Hay Bay church would have been a daily sight in his early years. His father, Hugh Macdonald, purchased a frame house from Paul Huff following the failure of his first venture in Canada, a store in Kingston. While Hugh tried to make a living by operating a store (which also failed) in one room of the house, young John went to school in

Adolphustown. The Macdonald house was located on a cove just across from the church.

In 1860, when the congregation built a new church in the next concession, the Hay Bay church fell into disrepair. In 1863 a visiting preacher described it in the *Christian Journal*: 'Neither shed nor tree, nor dwelling surround it. There it stands, silent and alone, hoary with years, stately in its ruin, and the centre and place of incidents and associations, which will outlive the transactions of Forums and Senates.'

For the next fifty years the building was used to store grain and farm implements. In 1910 the church and its nearby cemetery were purchased from the estate by which they were held and became the property of the Methodist Church. The building has since been carefully restored and cared for by the United Church of Canada. Travellers along the Bath Road would do well to journey a few miles north to view it.

The old Hay Bay Church, lot 18, concession 3, Adolphustown

Prince Edward County

To reach Prince Edward County by ferry is the surest way in which to sense its separation and its cohesiveness. The county is another world – a world tied with pride to its history. At the beginning of the nineteenth century a ferry was carrying passengers from Young's Point across the Adolphus Reach to Glenora. A ferry is still operating today.

There was likely a ferry at Glenora even before the Danforth Road was completed in 1801. It would have provided a necessary link between Prince Edward County and the centres of commerce to the east. The early ferries transported both people and cattle and were themselves propelled by horsepower – two horses on a treadmill.

For both the farmers in the county and those in the townships to the east, Glenora's main attraction was its mills. The first was built in 1796 by Peter Van Alstine, who had led the Loyalist settlers to Adolphustown. It stood on top of the cliff at Glenora. A few years later he built the mills that still stand below the limestone cliff, near the ferry landing, and in 1813 another, larger mill.

Peter Van Alstine was a fourth-generation American of Dutch descent. His family, like many others, was divided in its loyalties during the Revolution. Peter and two of his brothers maintained their allegiance to Britain while the other two brothers became colonels in the Revolutionary army. The trip to Upper Canada proved to be a difficult and hazardous one for the two hundred men, women, and children in the group he led. They suffered greatly during a long sea voyage from New York and a winter spent at Sorel, Quebec. Peter's wife died there. Within a few years of his arrival in the Quinte area, however, Van Alstine had become a leading figure and one of Upper Canada's first magistrates and legislators. Dr Canniff described him as fleshy, robust, dark-complexioned, extremely hospitable. 'No matter who came, he would order up from his cellar kitchen – the old Dutch style – his negro servants – slaves he had brought with him, and set before the traveller the necessary refreshments.'

The flour and carding mill at Glenora was operated from 1825 to 1836 by Hugh Macdonald, the father of John A. Young John received most of his schooling in Kingston, but it is likely that some of his holidays were spent at the Stone Mills. He once remarked: 'I had no boyhood. From the age of fifteen I began to earn my own living.' As a child, however, he probably spent some carefree time playing in the hills and valleys around Glenora.

One of the many stories told about the adult John A. Macdonald involves Glenora. In December 1851, he was campaigning for his seat in the legislature. He had earlier promised the Tory candidate in Picton that he would bring over all the Conservatives from Kingston who held property in Prince Edward County to vote there. Consequently he and three others arrived at Adolphus Reach, only to find that a storm had frozen the water and the ferry was immobilized. The ice was too thin to bear the weight of a sleigh or horses so, as Donald Creighton described in his biography of Macdonald, 'the cheerful and undaunted members of the voting party each secured two planks and, pushing these tentatively ahead, crawled slowly on their stomachs over the weakest part of the Reach towards the Stone Mills. There, a sleigh whisked them over the snowy road to Picton, and they cast their votes in time. Stevenson was elected. The entire Midland District had now been won for the Conservatives and the drive back to the Stone Mills was a triumphal progress.'

During the nineteenth century Stone Mills (Glenora) was a thriving community. After the War of 1812, the development of a large schooner fleet brought both markets and customers closer and encouraged industrial growth. A grist mill, a carding and fulling mill, a plaster mill, an iron foundry, a nail factory, and a horseshoe factory all were busy. For many years, too, the Little Giant Water Wheel Works manufactured turbines. During the first world war the foundry was turned into a munitions factory. It is now a fisheries research station under the Ministry of Natural Resources.

Just up the hill from the ferry dock stands the Stone Mills Stage and Ferry Hotel. It was built early in the century and served for many years as a stopping place for travellers along the Danforth. One of its owners, Jacob Adams, offered it for sale in 1831 with the following advertisement:

LOOK AT THIS

To be sold and possession given on the first of May next, the well known tavern situated near the Stone Mills in Marysburgh with the ferry across the bay of Quinty and 200 acres of excellent land. Its proximity to the Stone Mills and in the direct road from the thriving village of Hallowell to Kingston makes it a desirable stand for business.

In the 1890s the hotel was bought by John Green, the foreman of the iron foundry and owner of the ferry. During the following years, Green changed the building considerably. He removed some of the windows and fireplaces and added the large two-storey verandah seen today. The attractive barn to the west of the house was built around the turn of the century.

The Stone Mills Inn was in a key location as the first stop on the Danforth Road through Prince Edward County. The road continued through Picton, Bloomfield, Wellington, and Consecon to Carrying Place.

While many Quakers settled throughout Prince Edward County, the vast majority lived in Bloomfield, about four miles west of Picton on the Danforth. It was here that the first Quaker school was opened. Known as the West Lake Boarding School, it still stands on the north side of Highway 33, just east of the village (lot 13, concession 2, Military Tract). Some confusion exists as to the date of this building. Dr Canniff, in *A History of the Early Settlement of Upper Canada*, said that it opened in 1841 and was partially financed through the generosity of an English gentleman, John Joseph Gurney, the brother of Elizabeth Fry. He is said to have offered the Society £500 if they would raise the same amount. Registry Office records, however, show that the property did not come into the hands of the Society of Friends until 1848 and that in 1830 Israel

Bowrman, a Quaker, mortgaged the property for £500. It is possible that the mortgage money was used to build a house which later became the school. In any case, it is certain that the school operated for many years with a total enrolment of 110 pupils – not all housed in the one structure, for there were other buildings on the property at the time. The third storey of the house was a dormitory, the basement, which had a cooking fireplace, served as dining room and servants' quarters. The school even had indoor plumbing: the septic tank was built of red cedar logs, which are practically indestructible when buried. In 1865 the school closed down and moved to Pickering and then to Newmarket, where it became Pickering College.

Immediately to the west and also on lot 13, concession 2, Military Tract, is Fair Lea, the home of 'Squire' Thomas Morgan. The squire and his brother came to Upper Canada from Poughkeepsie after the War of 1812 and both bought farms near Bloomfield. Thomas Morgan prospered. He eventually owned two farms, a carding mill, and a

West Lake Boarding School, Bloomfield

sawmill, as well as the fine house which he built in 1834. Morgan was obviously a generous man for his name appears on the first subscription list for Victoria College in Cobourg as giving £30 – an impressive amount for the time. At his death in 1871, he left his wife Elizabeth 'my gold watch, the large clock now in my house, two beds and bedsteads, with all the bedclothing thereon, two bureaus, a rocking chair, parlour lookingglass and carpet, all she be at liberty to select for herself.' The high verandah on the front of his house adds a certain grandeur but was built later, and in error. Apparently a subsequent owner asked an architect friend to design a verandah for the house; the friend agreed, returned to his home in Kingston, and eventually mailed the drawings. But the plans he sent were meant for a different house, and by the time the mistake was discovered the verandah had been built.

Across from the Morgan house, on the south side of the road (lots 12 and 13, concession 2, Military Tract) is a red brick house. The

Fair Lea, home of Thomas Morgan, Bloomfield

first home on the property, as usual, was a log cabin. In 1810 the oldest part of the present structure was built, facing east. Then, in 1840, Benjamin Simpson built the large square brick house on the front of the earlier one and when it was completed added a formal garden surrounded by a picket fence. A centre driveway with a brick border led up to the house from an ornamental gate of iron and wood. Although the fence and gates have disappeared, some metal maple leaves have been found on the property of a type manufactured by McMullen's of Picton for ornamental fences.

Because Bloomfield was the heart of the Quaker settlement in Prince Edward County, it once had at least three meeting houses, each belonging to a different sect of the society. (The Quakers separated in 1828 into two branches, the liberal Hicksite Friends and the conservative Orthodox Friends. Fifty years later the second group suffered a further schism into 'progressive' and 'conservative' factions.) Unfortunately none of the buildings remain, although the Hicksite cemetery can still be seen at the west end of the village.

Just south of the cemetery is the home of one of the first Quaker families in the area, that of Elisha Talcott, his wife Sarah and their seven children. The house was built in 1862 and has remained in the family ever since. Most of the furniture in the parlour belonged to the builders and it is still in beautiful condition. Elisha Talcott was born in Connecticut but came to Prince Edward County with his family at the age of four. His house was built with bricks made on the property. Inside, it has some unusual features: large walk-in closets, uncommon at the time, second-storey windows that angle with the roof line, and a staircase whose bottom steps are splayed to one side. The house, like so many others of the period, had a verandah, and what is now a 'suicide door' in the front gable opened onto a small balcony set in the verandah roof. The family still has a bed stone, marked 'Sarah Talcott 1840,' which Sarah would have heated and used to warm her sheets. The date suggests that the Talcotts had an earlier, presumably simpler, dwelling.

On the Danforth west of Bloomfield is the village of Wellington, named of course, after the conqueror of Napoleon. The village possesses two outstanding houses at opposite extremes in design, each remarkable in its own way. In the eastern end of town, at 146 Main Street, is a magnificent and imposing house called Tara Hall. It stands on a rise overlooking the lake with a large expanse of lawn separating it from the road. Tara Hall was built by Archibald

McFaul, an Irishman who came to Wellington in 1815. Little is known of him but local historians suggest that he taught school for a while. It is known that he was involved in the drygoods business and exported grains and pork, and on one memorable occasion he acted as peacemaker in what the Hallowell *Free Press* of 15 January 1833 described as a 'New Year's Day Riot.' It began when 'a party of gentlemen met at Mr Wilman's hotel with the purpose of disecting a turkey and determining the merits of a few bottles of wine.' Between the party of 'our own towns people' and 'a party of Roman Catholics' a dispute took place.

The Romans met to the number of 10 or 12 at a private house and got drunk rather cheaper by purchasing wholesale than our Countrymen who met at the inn (very little credit attaches to either however). It appears from several circumstances that the Romans were very anxious for a blow or two just to keep their hand in; they began fighting at the bar-room door

Tara Hall, built by Archibald McFaul, 146 Main Street, Wellington

with 4 or 5 Canadians who were soon drove in the house by the enemy who were well provided with clubs and stones; no knives were used by them although they had them at hand. After the ground was cleared of the poor Canadians the enemy assailed the house with stones and bricks for some time when A. McFaul succeeded in getting them to leave the place. Isaac Huff is the only Canadian man that is dangerously wounded. Canadians submit to your masters and save your heads!

In 1832 McFaul bought property from William Maitland and Company, and five years later started construction of his house. The diary of an early settler, J. O'Brien Scully, records in November 1839 that 'Mr McFaul's new brick house, Tara Hall, was completed and he and his family went to reside there.' Eighteen years later the house and thirty-eight acres were sold by McFaul and wife to the Roman Catholic diocese of Kingston for £1,000. It would seem that McFaul's financial affairs had taken a turn for the worse. Perhaps he was never really able to afford a house of this size, for records show that he took out ten mortgages on some of his property in 1837, and in 1844 sold much of it to George Moffat to whom it appears he was in debt. McFaul lived in Wellington until his death in 1864.

While relatively little is known of the builder of Tara Hall, one thing is evident – he was a man of taste. Everything about the house confirms this. From the entrance hall with its vaulted ceiling to the curving staircase which leads to a magnificent ballroom on the second floor, every detail was carefully planned and executed. There are seven fireplaces, and only two of the mantels are the same. The wood trim throughout is beautiful. French doors lead into the ballroom from a wide hall which runs from east to west, unlike the back-to-front layout of similar houses. This was probably done to take advantage of the view. Even the small bedrooms show the same care in detailing. Tara Hall was neglected for many years but its present owner is gradually restoring it to its former grandeur.

While it may seem surprising that a house as elegant as Tara Hall was built in Wellington in 1837, it is equally unusual to find a house built about forty years earlier that is still in excellent repair. Few houses in Ontario have stood the rigours of time as well as the Daniel Reynolds house at 239 Main Street West, Wellington. It could be the oldest house between Kingston and Toronto. Stories abound about the Reynolds house, and all have improved with time. Reynolds came to Upper Canada from Albany, New York. He was a fur trapper and trader. According to some sources he built his house in 1786 with the help of Indians. This date is questionable, but it is a matter of record that he was married to Nancy Waite of Sophiasburg in 1792 and it is likely that he built his house shortly thereafter.

What really matters about the Reynolds house is its very presence after nearly two centuries. One-inch-square wooden pegs retain the floor boards, which are over one foot in width and two inches in depth. Hand-split lathes and hand-hewn eighteen-inch beams still do their work. The stone walls are over one foot thick. The small windows are typical of the period; the large ones are not and were added at a much later date. The house is divided by a central hall with one room on either side. Stairs lead up to what was probably an open loft; partitions were added some time later, as was

Daniel Reynolds house, built about 1792, 239 Main Street West, Wellington

an addition to the rear of the house. The house was heated by two large stone fireplaces. Originally the kitchen was in the basement and the bake oven and fireplace are still there. Settlers were aware of the importance of building foundation walls below the frost line, and basement kitchens were common. Often the settlers would live in the basement for a year or more until they were able to complete the rest of the house.

Further along Highway 33, west of the village of Hillier, on lot 26, concession 3, Hillier Township, is a simple brick farmhouse which has changed little from the time it was built in the middle of the nineteenth century. The house has its original windows. A belvedere lights the second-floor bedrooms. In houses with a hip roof it was necessary to provide either a belvedere or dormer windows to light the second storey. Dormer windows let the occupants see outside, but belvederes provided a neat appearance.

John Stapleton house, west of Hillier village, lot 26, concession 3, Hillier

This house was built (probably in the 1840s) by John Stapleton, who obtained the property from his mother and stepfather in 1831. Here he and his wife Jemima raised twelve children. John's father, William Stapleton, had come to Canada in 1776 from England. He was a master carpenter and for eighteen years served with the Queen's Regiment of Dragoons in that capacity at military posts in both Upper and Lower Canada. After his death in 1794, his widow re-married and with her new husband received the Crown grant for the property at Hillier in 1797. John Stapleton farmed the land successfully for many years. Along with his responsibilities at home he took up arms during the Rebellion of 1837, serving as a lieutenant in the 2nd Regiment of Prince Edward County. He died in 1853 at the age of fifty-six, but his wife lived for another thirty-nine years. In his will Stapleton left his property to two sons and it remained in the family until 1914.

The village of Consecon is situated on Weller's Bay adjacent to the present Highway 33. The main street of the village was the original Danforth Road. Its name Consecon was probably derived from an Indian word. For a time after 1832, the village was also called Marshtown, after the pioneer Marsh family.

Two fine early churches remain on the main street. The frame United Church (originally a Methodist chapel) was built about 1830. Even before church union in 1925 the Methodist and Presbyterian congregations of Consecon joined forces under its roof in an early example of ecumenism. The fieldstone Anglican church on Main Street, with its simple stonework and tower windows, was built in 1842.

Every traveller between Kingston and York was familiar with the Carrying Place. Even before the coming of the white man, the Indians portaged across it. Later, settlers along the north shore of Prince Edward County crossed the isthmus en route to the mills at Napanee. Once roads were built, the stage from York stopped there, its passengers changing to a steamboat for the remainder of the journey east. Just to the north of Carrying Place is the Murray Canal which was completed in 1890, allowing boats to pass from Lake Ontario to the Bay of Quinte.

The second man to settle in Carrying Place (the first being Colonel William Marsh) was Robert Young, a naval officer and a friend of John Graves Simcoe. The house he built in 1808 stands today on lot 1 southeast of Carrying Place, Ameliasburgh, just west of Highway 33.

Robert Young was born in Boston, the son of Scottish parents. At the outbreak of the American revolution he was in command of a British man-of-war. Early biographers say that he settled in Nova Scotia after the war, his first wife having died leaving him with two children, Joseph and Mary. However, since his first child by his second wife was born in Nova Scotia in 1773, it would appear that he moved there before and not after the Revolution. Young and his wife Jean produced a child nearly every other year until there were eight – suggesting, if nothing else, that he was not too far away for the duration of the war. By 1795, having heard of the fertile land and abundant game available in Upper Canada, he and his family decided to leave the Atlantic and the following year they settled at Carrying Place. The Crown patent for Young's house site was officially issued in 1807. In 1809 the 160 acres were transferred to

Robert Young house, Carrying Place

James Young, and in 1831 they passed by will to Reuben Young. During its early years the Young home was well known for the hospitality enjoyed there, and during the War of 1812 the land was a stopping place for troops. One account suggests that prisoners en route from Queenston Heights to Kingston were kept there. In 1822 Robert Young died. His children became prominent in military and political life and for many years were influential in the affairs of Prince Edward County and beyond.

The Young house is in amazingly good condition, particularly considering that it was built of wood. This may be due to the fact that it stayed in the family for more than one hundred and fifty years. Like the Reynolds house in Wellington, it had a basement kitchen. The small wing on the west side is a later addition and the verandah with its small enclosed porch appears to have been added later as well.

It would seem that the offspring of the more prominent pioneer families tended to marry those of similar social and economic background. Such was the case with Sarah Weller. She was the daughter of Asa Weller and Hannah Marsh, both of whose families prospered along the north shore of the lake. Asa Weller had founded a boat-hauling business at Carrying Place, carrying bateaux across the isthmus on rollers. His wife was the daughter of William Marsh, Sr, whose family had settled in Port Britain. Other members of the Weller family married into the Young family and the Proctor family of Brighton.

Sarah Weller, born in 1793, was the first white child born in Carrying Place. She married Richard John Neale Miskin and in 1828 they moved into the brick house on lots 8 and 9 southeast of Carrying Place, just a short distance east of the Youngs. The Crown patent for the land had been given to William Carl in 1809, but the property was sold to Eliakim Weller in the same year and Miskin bought it in 1825.

Originally a verandah stretched across the front of the house. When it was removed the stones from its foundations were used to build the little fence which now marks the front of the property. The kitchen wing, on the west side of the house, was built in 1869. Inside, the house has changed little over the years. The fireplace in what is now the dining room still has a swinging crane to hold the cooking pot. Many of the interior doors have small brass knobs typical of the period. The doors are panelled in the cross and bible pattern – a style referred to locally as 'witches' doors.'

From Picton, County Road 15 follows the shore of the Hayward Long Reach and cuts through the north part of Sophiasburg Township following the bay. It was opened in the early years of the 1800s as a military road. Where it crosses Highway 49 (lot 34, concession 1 southwest of Green Point) is an early Roblin house. This handsome stone building is now called The Chantry. It was built by Philip Roblin, Jr.

The Roblin family came to Upper Canada in the Loyalist party led by Peter Van Alstine that settled in Adolphustown. Philip's grandfather, John Roblin, died in 1788 and his widow and nine children moved to Sophiasburg, where they built a log house and grist mill. The township papers show an indenture dated 1794 concerned with the acquisition by John's son, Philip Roblin, Sr, of lot 33, concession 1, southwest of Green Point, Sophiasburg, which had a 'stream of water suitable for a mill or mills and also natural conveniences for erecting a Dam or Damms.' At this time Philip Sr also

Home of Sarah Weller and Richard Miskin, Carrying Place

owned part of lot 34, and acquired the rest of it in 1803. The land passed to his sons, Levi and Philip Jr, jointly in 1843, and all two hundred acres stayed in the family until the end of the century. Philip Jr built The Chantry on lot 34 about 1850.

The stones for The Chantry were cut by prisoners at the Kingston Penitentiary and brought by boat to Sophiasburg. A massive stone wall surrounded the property in 1850. The verandah on the front of the house was removed in recent years but otherwise the exterior is unchanged. Inside, two bedrooms were removed on the east side of the house to provide a larger living room and minor changes were made to adapt the house to present-day needs. The interior trim is the same as that in Tara Hall in Wellington.

Further up County Road 15, along what was once called the Marsh Front, are several houses built by descendants of the area's first settlers. In 1807 Abraham Cronk from Poughkeepsie purchased land (lots 5 and 6, concession 1 west of Green Point) in

The Chantry at Roblin Mills, County Road 15 and Highway 49

Sophiasburg from Tobias Ryckman. William Canniff reported that the purchase was made for half a barrel of salmon. The property passed in 1845 to James B. Cronk, who mortgaged it two years later. The sturdy stone house on the site today was probably built by Abraham and improved by James.

To the west of the Cronk land (on lot 11, concession 1 west of Green Point) stands a frame house. Pilasters frame each of its three doors and ornament the east and west ends of the façade. This is the Richard Solmes house, built for Richard's bride Lydia Cronk shortly after their wedding in 1813. Richard was the son of Nathaniel Solmes, who emigrated to Adolphustown at the end of the Revolutionary War. Nathaniel and his wife, Elizabeth Conklin, spent only two years there, however, and then bought lot 10, concession 1 west of Green Point. Richard purchased and built on the adjoining lot, and in 1831 was deeded his father's two hundred acres as well. At his death in 1867, Richard left only four acres of land to his eldest son,

Richard Solmes house, Sophiasburg

Reuben, and all the rest, including the beautiful house, to his other son, David. When Solmesville became a postal district and David the first postmaster, the frame dwelling assumed a new function. The old post office inkwells have remained in the house ever since.

In 1844 another frame house – similar in design and materials – was built on the Sophiasburg road three lots west of Richard and Lydia Solmes' home. It belonged to Richard Brooks and his wife Cynthia DeMille. Cynthia was the granddaughter of Isaac DeMille, who came up from Vermont in 1792. Immigration from the United States did not stop with the Loyalists. Some of the new arrivals were escaping persecution, which continued in the States even after the war when loyalty to Britain was suspected. Others were attracted by word of the good land and favourable settlement terms.

Set on what was initially an island stands an exceptionally beautiful stone house built by William Lazier (lot 18, concession 1 west of Green Point, Sophiasburg). The large front door has its original lock. The pine floors are beautifully preserved, showing rich colours and grain. In front of the fireplace, with its bake oven, is a floor of yellow ochre. The interior doors have small knobs, and the windows are deeply recessed.

William's Loyalist grandfather, Nicholas Lazier, came to Sophiasburg at the age of fifty-three, bringing with him his family and slaves. His son Nicholas, born in the United States in 1781, married Katherine Davenport, and obtained the Crown grant for lot 18 in 1802. The family had been millers in the United States and mill foundations at the back of the house indicate that they continued in this occupation in Sophiasburg. William, son of Nicholas and Katherine, built the present house in the 1830s to replace the first family home. The beauty of the building today is due in part to the cumulative effect of its detailing and in part to the careful attention of the present owners, whose insistence on authenticity included hand crafting of a pioneer tool with which to repair muntins, the slender wooden bars that separate the panes in windows.

During the first part of the nineteenth century, Quakers formed the largest single religious group in Prince Edward County. Before they were able to build a meeting house the Friends would hold meetings in the homes of members. Such meetings are recorded as early as 1784. In the north part of the county the earliest meetings were held in the Cronk house on lot 20, concession 1 west of Green

Point. It was built by Jacob Cronk, a young Quaker who arrived with his father Abraham well before the turn of the century. Early court records establish their presence in the area in 1793. In that year they had so good a crop that they stored one hundred bushels of wheat at the mill of John Walden Meyers of Meyers' Creek (Belleville). When the wheat was returned as flour the following spring, the Cronks believed there was less than there should have been. They sued. The judges awarded them £2.7.6.

Abraham Cronk was among the early settlers who brought slaves to their new country. But slave-owning did not necessarily mean that a family was wealthy. In order to finance a trip to the United States to bring back his bride, young Jacob had to sell part of his land and spend the winter working in Adolphustown cutting cordwood for four dollars a month plus board. His trip was successful, however, and her name, Anna Cronk, can still be seen scratched in the glass in one of the windows of their house.

William Lazier house, overlooking the Bay of Quinte, Sophiasburg

The Quaker meetings, which were held in the Cronk house as early as 1808, took place upstairs. There were originally two doors leading from the outside to the second floor, one at the west end and one at the rear; it seems likely that these doors provided the separate entrances for men and women that were customary in Quaker meeting houses. The 1798 journal of Rufus Hall (a Philadelphia Quaker) refers to a visit with the Cronks. Another account of a meeting of the Society of Friends in the house was provided by Phoebe Roberts, a Quaker missionary, who wrote in her diary after visiting there on 5 November 1821:

Set out at two o'clock, travelled 16 miles up the Bay of Quimby, a great water, and attended a meeting that was appointed for us at six in the evening, at Jacob Cronk's house. This meeting is called the Green Point Meeting. There was a large gathering of Friends and others ... Jacob Cronk and his wife are Germans, valuable Friends, both members of the select meeting. They have one son whose name is Samuel, their only child, a worthy young man and his wife a precious little woman. They were very wealthy people and appeared to live in much harmony.

Jacob and Anna's son, Samuel, predeceased them. After his death in 1841, Jacob wrote a will leaving all the property to Samuel's son, Jacob S. Cronk, except for the furniture and the east half of the house. These he left to his wife to share with their daughter-in-law, Eliza. This arrangement explains the two doors at the front of the house; one led to the grandson's half, the other to the part occupied by the women. The exterior wood has been replaced on the front of the house but the original hand-planed siding is in remarkable condition on the sides and back.

Daniel Way, the first of another local family, was a rarity in Prince Edward County: he had fought in the American militia during the Revolution. After the war he converted to the Quaker faith and to the British Crown. His father disinherited him for becoming a Quaker, giving him only '£5 as his birthright.' Daniel travelled to Upper Canada with his wife, Jemima Kilburn, and his sons, James and Samuel. James married Sarah, the daughter of the Abraham Cronk who had built the stone house at the east end of the Sophiasburg road. For her he built another stone house on lot 15, next to his father on lot 16, both concession 1 west of Green Point.

Samuel, Daniel Way's other son, in 1802 received a Crown grant for 342 acres of lot 24, concession 1, further west along the road. On a site which possessed the natural beauty of inlets fronting on the bay, Samuel built a simple rubblestone cottage. It had two bedrooms, a summer kitchen, a woodshed and a kitchen-living area, but no basement or attic. Eighteen-inch windows are close to the ceiling, with supporting timber beams above. A dormer filled the second level. The Ways used stone in their homes partly because of its availability and partly as a continuation of a tradition, for stone-masonry had been the family trade in the United States. In 1818 Samuel was killed by a falling tree on a visit to Hillier Township. His son, Daniel Samuel, carried on in his father's home until his mother's death and then sold the property to Isaac Morden in 1832.

Morden built the two-storey building which forms the west side of the present complex. He used fine-cut stone, and brought limestone lintels and fine hardware from Kingston. The new structure was intended to be a wedding gift for Isaac's son, William, but when the

Quaker Meeting House, the Jacob Cronk home, Sophiasburg

young man died suddenly it became the home of Isaac's daughter, Nancy Morden Wilson. The beautiful main door is now protected by a portico which was added in recent years. When the portico was built, the roof of the main house was raised and a second storey added to the original cottage.

The circumstances by which Daniel Way arrived in Canada are in marked contrast to the story of Henry Redner, a supporter of the Crown who was shot and wounded in his New Jersey home by Revolutionary soldiers, had his property confiscated, and was forced to leave the United States. Redner travelled with the Loyalists from New York, wintered in Sorel, and journeyed to Adolphustown township by bateau. His tale was not unique. It was the pattern for many hundreds of settlers, but no less difficult for that. Stories told to succeeding generations of the Redner family recalled the hardships of pioneering by Lake Ontario, including the Hungry Year (1798) when they were forced at times to depend on berries.

Home of James Redner, Rednersville, Ameliasburgh

Henry Redner had a son named Henry (as well as four other children, John, Peter, Maria, and Sophia). That Henry also had a Henry (as well as James and Phoebe). This gave great family continuity but causes much confusion in attempts to follow the movements of the various namesakes.

In 1802 the Crown patents for lots 76 and 77, concession 1, Ameliasburgh were issued to Henry Redner, Jr, the son of the pioneer. This land included much of the site of what would be called Rednersville. In the 1840s his son James built the stone house that still stands on the south side of the road in the western end of the village. It replaced an early log building, and was constructed almost entirely with materials at hand. The stone was cleared from the farm land; the lumber was cut at the site; the lime used to form plaster was made there as well. All the interior woodwork was hand carved.

James Redner owned the store in the village and rented it to the postmaster. He also ran a successful business buying grain and shipping it from a nearby wharf, storing it in his warehouse prior to shipping. In 1850 he undertook the postmaster's duties in addition to his other activities.

James was married twice but had no children. His brother Henry eventually took over the house and expanded it to accommodate his own children – adding the peaked gable, and by raising the roof securing two more bedrooms. A verandah which was originally part of the house was later removed.

3

Picton

The settlement on the west side of the creek at the head of Picton Bay was known as Hallowell Bridge until 1837. In that year it was forced to relinquish its name in favour of that of the settlement east of the creek, named like the bay after Sir Thomas Picton, a British general of the Napoleonic Wars. The Hallowell *Free Press* was full of lively letters commenting on the change of name.

The west-of-the-creek settlers were possibly reluctant to give up their association with Benjamin Hallowell, a UEL with a colourful series of brushes with the Revolutionaries. He had been a commissioner of customs at the port of Boston in the dangerous times of the Boston Tea Party, and, realizing that he was high on the rebel list of targets, had departed for England. Thereupon he was 'banished' from the United States somewhat after the fact, and his lands and holdings in Maine were confiscated. Eventually he was granted land in Nova Scotia and Prince Edward County.

The small community of Hallowell Bridge met regularly to discuss problems after 1800. The three-storey building at 64 Bridge Street, then Thomas Eyre's inn, is believed to have been the location of many of these meetings. Its location on the Danforth Road at the bridge would have made it the obvious spot for the refreshment of travellers and the transaction of business. The inn was constructed of stone with rough cast over. The lower level was the servants' quarters and the kitchen area. Stables and yards were on the west side.

The Eyre property was part of a Crown grant made to nine-year-

old William Macaulay in November 1803. Its sale to Eyre was recorded in September 1816, but Eyre could have been renting the land before then. Old documents refer to an Eyre's Inn in 1807. It is difficult to date the building exactly. Certainly stone, of which it was constructed, was readily available at that date; however, there may have been an earlier inn of logs on the same site. Whatever the exact date, there is no doubt that the present building was a focus of community life at the beginning of the nineteenth century. When Thomas Eyre died in September 1847, in his eighty-second year, the Hallowell *Free Press* commented: 'Mr. Eyre was one of the first if not the first settler in the limits of the present town of Picton. He came here in 1791 and was for a long time the landlord of the only Inn at the head of the bay ... From that time until the day of his death, a period of over 50 years, Mr Eyre was noted for his strict honesty and punctuality in all his business transactions ... a worthy sample of the old stock of settlers who in the lapse of time have mostly given place to a new generation – and we wish we might add – to a better!'

William Macaulay, who had been given the Crown grant for what became the Eyre lands, had other extensive holdings on the east side of Hallowell Bridge. It was he, in the 1830s, who favoured the name of Picton. William was a son of Robert Macaulay of Ireland, who emigrated to America in 1764, spent six months in the Albany jail during the Revolution for aiding the British, was released on bail, and escaped to Canada. William went to Oxford, became a deacon in 1818, and in the next year was ordained and assigned to Cobourg. He became rector of Old St Mary's, Picton, in 1827 and remained there until 1874. According to Bishop Strachan's journals, Macaulay built both the church and the rectory at Picton largely at his own expense, the church alone costing £1200. Macaulay married Anne Catherine Geddes and, after her death in 1849, Charlotte Sarah Vesconte. The Macaulay papers in the Ontario Archives contain many letters to his mother describing his life, work, and marriage. On 1 September 1829, he wrote:

I find myself very happily married to a wife, who I trust will unite affection and prudence in her conduct as respects myself and who will be doubly dear to me, if she answers as I trust she will the expectation that I have

Thomas Eyre's inn, 64 Bridge Street

that she will be an excellent and dutiful daughter-in-law. Our little cottage is a very comfortable one.

The Macaulay's little cottage was their first home, in which they lived until the stone and brick rectory was completed around 1830. The rectory, at 35 Church Street, is located just west of the Old St Mary's Church. Originally it had a small portico at the front; this was removed in 1850 and replaced with a verandah which sheltered the front at the first storey level. This was in turn removed in 1975 and a portico re-installed as in the original design. Pegged beams, square nails, and a bake oven indicate the age of the house. The basement, which held a well-stocked wine cellar, has the original floor, part dirt, part brick, part stone. The house is being carefully restored.

Old St Mary's (originally called St Mary Magdalene) is located at the corner of Church and Union Streets. It was built in 1823 of

The rectory of Old St Mary's

cream-coloured brick which was made locally. An organ was installed in 1854 and is still in the building. The chancel was added in 1864. From 1913 to 1970 the church stood empty. Then Prince Edward County became its owner and restored it, highlighting the simple beauty of the early small-paned cathedral windows. The building is now a museum.

The graves of many early settlers may be found in Old St Mary's cemetery but one stone attracts more attention than others. Ever since it was reported in Ripley's 'Believe It or Not,' visitors have come considerable distances to see the tablet of a man who achieved fame by dying on a day that never dawned. The gravestone is inscribed: 'Wm. Pierce, Died Feb. 31, 1860. Aged 73 years.'

Set back on the west side of Union Street stands a building which caused much dissension between Hallowell and Picton at the time of its construction – the Prince Edward County Court House. When plans were being made for it, the obvious question arose: on which

Old St Mary's Church

side of the stream should it stand? Macaulay exerted his considerable influence in favour of Picton. The fact that his strong views
were backed by a financial contribution caused considerable comment from the Hallowell side. There was no argument, however,
about the need for the building, wherever it stood. Until it was built,
court business involved a rigorous journey to Kingston, whether it
was a prisoner waiting for commitment or an innkeeper seeking a
license.

The court house was completed in 1834. It is built of dressed
limestone. Its façade is as formidable as halls of justice should be,
yet its architecture is strikingly beautiful. The fine door is the
recent work of Prince Edward County – an exact replica of the
original. The windows are of the early twelve-over-twelve style.
The cupola was added in the 1860s. The site, so imposing today, was
denounced at the time by 'A Voice Of The Public' in the Hallowell
Free Press of 12 April 1831 as 'in the vicinity of accumulating

Prince Edward County Court House, Union Street

graveyards ... and stagnant mill ponds ... and marshes with noxious effluvia.'

The jail behind the court house was built in 1860. It had eighteen cells measuring 8 feet × 3 feet × 12 feet high, and four special detention cells which the light of day never penetrated. The women had slightly roomier cells and these, painted pink, are still used upon occasion today for members of both sexes. In 1884 the Court House was the scene of a double hanging, and for that purpose a double gallows was built of oak. There had been a murder in Bloomfield and two local men, Joseph Tompsett and George Louder, were convicted. (The murder house still stands near Bloomfield with a famous bullet hole in the door.) The execution was bungled. Those present were horrified when Tompsett took fourteen minutes to die because the noose slipped. Later, doubt arose as to the actual guilt of the pair buried in the jailyard. A letter was found from Tompsett proclaiming his innocence:

Dear kind and loving mother, these my last and dying words. I never new that fatal shot was fired nor that man was killed nor nothing of that murder nor my boots never made them tracks but the jury says I must die to pay some mans penalty. I am ready to die but I die for something I never don.

A letter from Louder to the people of the county was published after his death with similar protestations. Claims of manufactured evidence, mistaken identity, evidence mysteriously held back, and confusing footprints in the snow served to keep the subject alive. The double gallows still stands behind the women's cells.

A copy of a bill dated 11 June 1884 was found recently, itemizing the expenses of the execution:

To expense of self and H.V.Carson to Kingston and return to take plans of the Kingston scaffold $7.50

H.V. Carson a/c for building and furnishing material for scaffold as per a/c and voucher attached $33.35

James Hart a/c material for Blk. flag and cape .69

F. Wood a/c making Blk cap .25

J.N. Carter a/c for rope $1.05

R.D.H. a/c printing copies of certificate of Surgeon, Declaration of Sheriff and others and Inquest $5.00

Paid Hangman $40.00

Refreshments for Hangman $6.50

On the east side of Picton Bay, at 115 Bridge Street, is a single-storey stone house built shortly after 1812 by Elephalet Adams, a relative of John Quincy Adams of Massachusetts, sixth president of the United States. Adams was born at Ringe, New Hampshire, in 1775, but emigrated to Canada and in 1805 married eighteen-year-old Mary Washburn. From the stone cottage he conducted a successful lumbering and building business. When he died in 1816, he left an estate worth £1,567, including household goods totalling £68 in value: 'one dozen half large plates, one dozen cups sasers, one salt seler, one muster pott, one dozen soop plates, one half dozen boles large, two chamber pots, shuger bole and one sass boat, one white wash bole and two beds and bedding.' The windows at the front of his cottage have been altered and replaced with larger panes, but those on the sides of the house retain the original smaller ones.

Mary Washburn Adams was the daughter of Ebenezer Washburn, formerly of Worcester, Massachusetts. Washburn had fought

115 Bridge Street, built by Elephalet Adams

for the Crown, been captured and imprisoned at Saratoga when Burgoyne was defeated in 1777, escaped, and joined Jessup's Corps. Later he went to Sorel, and then on to Prince Edward County where he chose land in Hallowell. Accompanying him was his bride, the former Sarah de Forest, a relative of Laura Secord. The Ebenezer Washburn home, a two-storey brick building built in 1814, stands at 339 Main Street. It is now the rectory of the new Church of St Mary Magdalene, its neighbour to the south. The panelling of its main entrance door is noteworthy.

The house at 103 Bridge Street is built of board and batten and has a mansard roof – both unusual features in the area. (Settlers in Prince Edward County usually chose stone or brick as building materials because they would endure.) The south side originally housed a conservatory; French doors opened onto a verandah at the front. The house was built in the 1870s by Maxwell Lepper, an Anglican minister, using plans brought from Ireland. By that time the

Board and batten, 103 Bridge Street

property had passed through many hands – from Deborah Ellsworth who received the Crown grant in 1803, to Thomas Eyre in 1813, to his descendants, and from them to Rev. William Macaulay in 1869. Lepper purchased the property in 1874 and probably built the house that year. It is interesting primarily because of its style and because it is in such good condition for a frame building.

Sometimes a figure from the early 1800s appears, through his home and through early records, as a man of mystery even though there may be considerable documented record of his activities. Such a man is Philip Low, the owner of Castle Villeneuve on Picton Bay. Belden's *Historical Atlas of Hastings and Prince Edward Counties* identifies Low as a native of Jersey, one of the Channel Isles; through his mother he was connected with Admiral Villeneuve, who commanded the French fleet against Nelson at Trafalgar. After studying law, he settled in 1834 in Picton, where he became county crown attorney and mayor. During the Mackenzie rebellion he commanded a section of loyal soldiers in the battle of Montgomery's Tavern. He must have been aggressive, imaginative, and a man of vision for, according to Belden, he originated the laying of a submarine cable across the Bay of Quinte in 1855. He was then president of the Grand Trunk Telegraph Company, which he founded; the company had sixty-six offices and lines from Quebec to Buffalo, with branches to Peterborough and Barrie – 'These towns undoubtedly owed their early telegraphic facilities solely to the energy and enterprise of Mr Low.' Low also established the Bank of Montreal in Picton, was a major in the militia, and operated a flaxmill.

When he first came to Picton, Low lived in a white frame house which he bought or built at the corner of Bridge and Low streets. In 1840 he bought a simple farmhouse, built twenty years earlier by James Cummings on the north side of Bridge Street, and gradually embellished it. To the original austere exterior he added, over a period of years, wings, turrets, fanciful towers, gothic windows, a cupola, and a heavy entrance door. The ornaments were a conspicuous reflection of his financial success. In his will, Low left his entire fortune to his children, 'being satisfied that ... they will make due provision for my wife.'

There is a family connection between the red brick Georgian house at 353 Main Street East and the commercial building at 237 Main Street. Both were at one time associated with Gideon Striker, druggist, Reformer in politics, and three-time MLA for the district.

The house was built in 1868; the date is executed in wrought iron under the eaves at the front of the house. That was the year in which Striker bought the property from Jacob Johnson, whose family had owned the land for sixty-two years. Striker's success in trade is evident in the quality of materials used in building his home. The good brick has weathered beautifully and is accented by exceptionally fine wrought iron work which draws attention to the French windows and dignified doorway.

Striker was a justice of the peace and lieutenant-colonel of the reserve militia. Belden's *Atlas* described him in 1878 as 'ernest, energetic and consistent.' His ancestor, James Striker, had come from Duchess County, New York; according to Belden's writer, James had been arrested by the Continental authorities and charged with harbouring spies: 'He was tried by drum-head court-martial, found guilty and sentenced to be executed for the same; and the carrying-out of the sentence was only prevented by the violent in-

Castle Villeneuve on Picton Bay

terposition of an influential officer of high rank, who was a relative and great personal friend of Mr Striker ... the incident had the effect of hastening his departure to this refuge of his majesty's loyal subjects.'

The Chapman and Striker pharmacy is reputed to be the oldest pharmacy operating in Ontario. It was founded in 1829 by R.J. Chapman, who came from New York State bringing his apothecary scales with his other moveables. The first issue of the Hallowell *Free Press*, 4 January 1831, carried his notice:

R.J. Chapman begs to announce to his friends and the public generally that he has lately opened a shop one door east of the brick building occupied by Messrs Foster and Ellison where he intends keeping on hand a general and extensive assortment of:– Drugs, medicine and perfumery, Also groceries of every description among which will be found the following; Teas, sugars, liquors, wines, port and L.P. Teneriffe, cogniac brandy, Jamaica spirits,

353 Main Street East, once the home of Gideon Striker

shrub and peppermint, Gunpowder, mackerell, codfish, herring, candles and soap. Wanted: 200 bushels of good oats. R.J. Chapman, Hallowell, Dec. 28, 1830.

After the business was well established, Chapman invited Gideon Striker, who was his brother-in-law, to join with him and they continued together until 1873. The drug store is located in an exceptionally fine commercial building on Main Street. High windows topped with eared architraves are balanced on either side of narrow central windows with finely carved ornamentation.

Walter Ross, from Aberdeen, is credited with the construction of the brick house at 347 Main Street East. Built in the 1850s, it was the home during his Picton years of George McMullen, the man who sparked the Pacific Scandal that toppled Sir John A. Macdonald. McMullen came of a Picton family (the 1851 census for Canada West listed both Daniel McMullen, a farmer born in Nova Scotia, Wesleyan Methodist, and his son George, then eight years old) but moved to Chicago and the wider world of business, finance, and power. When Canada was planning its first transcontinental railway, he and a group of wealthy American businessmen attempted to convince the Macdonald government that they should receive the contract. They represented the Northern Pacific Railway and hoped to make the Canadian railway part of the American scene; that a central part of the line would run through the northern United States was a feature they did not advertise. When they were rejected they came back with another proposal, similar, but with a Canadian, Sir Hugh Allan, at the head and the Americans very much in the background. Allan received the government's eventual approval but without any American involvement. During the negotiations, however, the Americans had advanced money through Allan to Macdonald and other Conservatives to help finance their campaign in the 1872 elections. McMullen threatened to disclose this information if Macdonald did not grant him and his partners railway concessions, and when the prime minister refused incriminatory documents were in fact made public. The resulting controversy destroyed Allan and the first Canadian Pacific Railway company and drove Macdonald from office and very nearly ended his political career.

At the time the Picton papers spoke with disdain of McMullen's role in the affair. The *Gazette* remarked on 1 August 1873 that,

'Having tried the role of informer and retailer of private correspondence, McMullen has earned for himself an unenviable reputation and has forfeited all claims for respect at the hands of those who prize honour and virtue.' Nevertheless, McMullen returned to Picton and the Main Street house. He subsequently became a prime mover of the Prince Edward County Railroad and manufactured a unique and very Canadian product – a fence whose vertical stays of woven wire were each topped with a maple leaf. Such fences were common in the county in the 1880s.

Of all the products which early settlers produced for practical household as well as commercial use, the pottery crock is one of the most aesthetically pleasing. The town of Picton was known through a wide area of Upper Canada in the mid-nineteenth century as the home of the Hart pottery works. Its grey-beige crocks with blue designs, which have become collectors' items, were formed, fired,

Hove-To, home and site of the pottery works of the Hart and Lazier families

and glazed at Hove-To on Main Street East (on a site between the present hospital and golf course). The pottery operated under various trade names over the years.

The Hart family came from Kent in England and emigrated to Fulton, New York – first Samuel Hart in 1828, then his brother James in 1830, and finally their sister Mary and her husband, Charles Skinner, in 1836. The success of the pottery works they founded at Fulton led younger members of the family to seek new areas in which to establish a business. In 1849 Samuel Skinner (the son of Mary and Charles) bought land in Picton. In the same year another member of the second generation, William Hart, became part owner of the business along with his uncle Samuel.

Their firm was known as William Hart and Co. from 1847 to 1855, during which time the frame house and work buildings were most probably built. Now only the house and one outbuilding remain. Exactly who had the house built is not known, for at the time the land was owned jointly by William Hart and Samuel Skinner. It has been kept in excellent condition; the chief alteration has been the relocation of the main entrance, which originally led directly into the central room and now is at the side of the porch. The floor plan is unusual in its asymmetrical layout, and local authorities feel that it must have been patterned after the Hart home in Fulton. The layout gives an easy flow from room to room, and the beautifully worked interior trim and large fireplaces create that nebulous warm atmosphere which some houses seem to possess.

In 1855 William Hart sold his part of the business. The company was thereafter managed in Picton by Samuel Skinner, and the crockery bore the mark S. Skinner and Co. The clay for the crocks and the salt for glazing were imported from New York, and delivered to a wharf at the foot of the property. The manufacture – mixing, shaping, firing, and glazing – was completed on the property, and many crocks were personalized with merchants' names.

The property and business changed hands once more within the family in 1874. Alcena Hart and her husband, George Lazier, lived in the house and ran the business as Hart and Lazier. After George's death, Alcena and her brothers expanded the business to Belleville; but in 1892 the property was sold to R. Metcalf and after forty-three years in business the pottery closed.

The White Chapel, two miles north of Picton on Highway 49 at County Road 6, epitomizes in its construction the best of the pioneer life style and character – co-operation, joint enterprise, and pride of workmanship. In 1809 Stephen Conger, a mill owner, gave land and lumber for the construction of what is now one of the oldest United churches in Canada. All the other members of the congregation gave what they could in money, materials, and labour. (One of the first adherents was Sal, a slave owned by Nicholas Lazier.) Solidly built of frame, well and sensibly furnished inside with the finest materials skilfully worked, the chapel today is still in excellent condition. It is also a reminder of the colourful and controversial Methodist saddle-bag preachers who, armed with the Bible and an eloquent tongue, a black cloak, and a broad brimmed hat, spread evangelism, formed classes, and conducted meetings in the wilderness.

To see the large solid early bricks on the side and back of the Arra Ferguson house at 23 Ferguson Street is to come full circle to the first buildings in Hallowell Bridge. When, on 26 October 1816, Fer-

The White Chapel outside Picton, one of the oldest Methodist chapels in Canada

guson and his wife received the Crown patent for the property, he was already contributing to the life of Hallowell; between 1812 and 1830, he served as the elected town clerk for all but four years. Early records list only two brick houses in Hallowell in 1818: the Ferguson house could have been one of them. Its bricks have the attractive roughness and uneven line of the hand-made product. In 1823 the house was owned by Ira Spafford, and one year later it was the property of John McQuaig. By 1852, when it became the property of Gideon Striker, it had also belonged to John and Joseph Trumpour, Simeon Washburn, Peter McGill, and John Platt Williams. Many of the prominent names in Picton's history have connections with this old brick building.

Newspapers and letters from the 1830s and 1840s fill in the small details of life in Picton at the time. Rev. William Macaulay wrote to his brother John of a cholera epidemic in August 1834. 'It is said that

23 Ferguson Street, the Arra Ferguson house built of large, handmade bricks

a case of cholera occured yesterday at Demorestville and that Nelson ... was seized with it today. We must be prepared for the worst.' '8 pm ... I hear of 29 deaths yesterday, Dr Robinson being particularly mentioned.'

In September 1847, Macaulay remarked in a letter to his mother: 'The electric telegraph seems to be extending itself everywhere. The world will get all its news now at once, which will not be half so pleasant as when it came driblet by driblet after long expectation – Indeed what with steam boats, rail cars, electric telegraphs and so forth the next generation will be altogether a different kind of race from our dull plodding generation.'

On 6 December 1831, the Hallowell *Free Press* commented: 'Among the numerous bad habits to which many men in our village and town are addicted we would particularly notice the practice of horse racing which occurs in our streets almost every day and night ... At present a lady cannot even cross the street in the evening without exposing herself to the danger of being run over by horses that have had their spirits raised from the few drops of Bacchus which their riders have taken before leaving a bar room.'

In June 1833 the Hallowell *Free Press* announced the forthcoming arrival of a circus which would include 'a fully grown male elephant, the Royal Bengal Tiger (as large as a lion, perfectly vicious) and a beautiful African Leopard.' As remarkable as the animals was the feat of transporting them over roads which were always in bad condition. When coaches and sleighs had difficulty, it takes some imagination to picture a fully grown elephant reaching Hallowell.

During the circus performance, the keeper entered the leopard's cage – an act of considerable daring according to the newspaper since 'It has been common in all ages, for the keepers to enter the dens of lions with safety. But the treacherous Leopard has not (until the present instance) submitted to this degree of familiarity.' The attempt was made without mishap in Hallowell. Five months later, the *Free Press* reported: 'It is stated that the keeper of the tigers belonging to the extensive menagerie which was exhibited in this town a few months since was torn to pieces and literally eaten up by them a few days since, in a town near New-Haven, Connecticut.'

4

Cataraqui-Odessa

Waterloo, now Cataraqui Village, reached a population peak of three hundred by the 1870s; Dr Canniff described it as 'a very pretty and neat little hamlet' with a town hall, church, stores, and inns. Its central feature was and is the Cataraqui cemetery. Canniff speculated that the sixty-five acres, 'when ornamented by such numerous and elegant monuments, as the living have erected to mark their respect to the beloved dead in older places of sepulture, will be unsurpassed by the oldest and most beautiful cemeteries known.' Today the cemetery shows its age not only in the dates on its gravestones but also in the size and beauty of its trees. Sir John A. Macdonald is buried here, his grave marked by a small stone surrounded by a wrought iron fence. The location certainly does not force itself upon the visitor.

Near the eastern gates of Cataraqui cemetery, at 911 Purdy's Mill Road, is a limestone schoolhouse (now a land surveyor's office) which was one of the first such buildings in the area. The address recalls a mill at the end of the road which was operated by the descendants of Gilbert Purdy, Jr, one of Michael Grass's party of Loyalists. The family settled along the Bath Road and in Cataraqui, where they owned the small mill houses near the schoolhouse and co-operated in a brick business owned by Johnson Day.

Limestone was the obvious choice as a building material in this area, its chief assets being that it was readily available, uniform in colour, and virtually ageless. Its use was also appropriate for simple designs such as that of the schoolhouse, which relies entirely on its cupola for ornamentation.

Across the road from the Purdy property, at 2263 Princess Street, is a building which is reported to have been built for its doctor-owner, William Beamish, using stone quarried by convict labour. Beamish had been licensed to practice medicine in Upper Canada in 1830 and three years later began purchasing parts of lot 15, concession 2, Kingston Township, the site of the present building. Over thirty years he made seven separate purchases – one of them from a fellow physician, Dr Horace Yeomans, who had been in the village since 1819. It is believed that Beamish built his large stone house in 1859, employing convicts who could be otained for twenty-five cents a day. The stone came from a Collins Bay quarry.

Beamish also is reported to have served as a doctor at the penitentiary. He would have been a youngish man when the first prison opened in 1836, and his cases might well have included prisoners who had been subjected to excessive flogging – an abuse which caused a public outcry in the next year. He might also have treated the chil-

The old school house, Cataraqui Village

dren who were detained in the prison, and whose youth did not exempt them from flogging at as tender an age as eight. The penitentiary policy included a 'prison worker contract system' which allowed prisoners to be used as cheap labour in competition with skilled local artisans. Many houses in the district were built by their efforts. The policy was reviewed in the 1850s, and Dr Beamish's house would have been one of the last to be constructed in this way. Beamish sold the property in 1870. In 1904 it became the rectory for Christ Church, Cataraqui, and has subsequently served as a private home and an architect's office.

Sproul's Farmers and Drovers Inn (lot 3, concession 3, Kingston) was the centre of activity in the growing village of Westbrook in 1857, when it was listed in the *Kingston Directory* along with the Sproul and Company Co. Saw Mill. The inn, a simple, utilitarian, two-storey limestone building, has deteriorated since its days of importance on the Kingston Road, but it retains clues, in the placing of

William Beamish house, 2263 Princess Street, Cataraqui Village

its windows and the second-floor doorway that once opened onto a verandah, of its original function.

To the west (lot 4), the William Marshall family farmed the land. In building their stone house, the Marshalls altered the standard window design by adding side lights to the normal central fifteen-pane section.

William Marshall also owned the part of lot 4 which lay south of the York-Kingston road, having purchased it from the Crown gran-tee, Eliza Taylor, in 1840. In 1860 Marshall sold that one-sixth of an acre to the Wesleyan Methodist congregation, who quickly built a stone church on it. The building served as a centre of worship for only five years, however. Then a new church, now Westbrook United, was opened on the north side of the highway, further east in town. The original church building has since served as a church hall, a school, a union hall, and finally a private residence. Sturdily built, with walls two feet thick, it retains the appearance of its first role,

Sproul's Farmers and Drovers Inn, Westbrook

with its enclosed porch and gothic doors facing the road. Inside many of the original features remain – the vaulted ceiling, large beams, pine floor boards, and hardware. The recessed nine-foot cathedral windows have wide single-plank pine sills.

An intriguing name commemorating a Russian city, a romantic Regency cottage, a stone mill, and a wealthy miller's residence – these are part of Odessa, a pleasant but little-known village on the old stage route. Odessa's most famous landmark, the stage coach inn with its ornate two-storey verandah is gone but is not lost, for the front of the structure was rescued, repainted, and stands upright in the old Lennox and Addington County Jail, now a museum.

Odessa owed its development as a commercial, self-supporting village in large measure to the Booth family, descendants of Joshua Booth, a Loyalist who settled on the Bath Road. Joshua established the family in the milling business: at Millhaven he opened the first grist mill in Ernestown Township. Benjamin, his son, moved to Mill Creek, later called Odessa, and took over the mills of John Link. In succeeding years various members of the Booth family owned stores and factories in Odessa as well as the original mills.

South on Factory Road in the village are four buildings associated with the Booth family – the old planing mill, the woollen mill, and two houses. On the east side of the road, across from the mill, is a handsome limestone house, built into the bank so that it is a storey lower on the side facing the stream than it is at the front. In 1803 Joshua Booth received this property from the Crown and it remained in the family for one hundred and four years until it was purchased by John Herbert Babcock. Benjamin Booth inherited the site after Joshua's death in 1813. He took out a mortgage on the property in 1820 which could mean that a house was then being constructed, but that building was probably replaced by the present stone dwelling in 1840.

West of the miller's house, the remains of the Booth milling complex can be seen. A grist mill was the first of the group to be built, in 1820. It has disappeared, as has a sawmill which stood until 1940. The woollen mill remains near the house and on its west side the planing mill stands at the edge of the creek. At one time a basket factory was located on the mill's second floor.

In 1842 Benjamin Booth deeded the mill property to his sons Philip and John K. Booth, retaining for himself the woollen mill by the house and two acres of land. In the conditions of the deed Benja-

min stipulated that Philip and John pay £225 to James and Donald Booth (relationship uncertain) when they came of age and 'decently cloth and also wash and mend for them until they come of age or until they wish to go to themselves.' Philip and John were also obligated to decently clothe, feed, and house their father, 'also wash and mend for him during his natural life and should the said Benjamin Booth have just cause to be dissatisfied with the treatment, they are to pay to him ... thirty-seven pounds ten shillings per year.'

John Booth located his home on Factory Road near the woollen mills and south of the mill house site, in the Irish section of town. The Irish community, who built their houses south and east of the village centre, may have been employed in the construction of the Napanee-to-Kingston macadamized road. They called Booth's house Skibereen Castle, a pretentious name for a middle-class intruder.

Wesleyan Methodist Church, Westbrook, now a private residence

Skibereen Castle, home of John Booth

Skibereen is a market town in County Cork. The house was built around 1838 and its stone walls were eighteen inches thick. They have been stuccoed over by a later owner. The pine floors remain, as do the original carved baseboards and woodworking around the doors. There was no fireplace; the house was undoubtedly heated by a large wood stove. Booth would probably have been more popular if he had built a new tavern to add to the five already in the area.

Philip Booth, born in Ernestown, came to Odessa with his father. He later developed the lumbering business and the grist mill in the family name. He may have lived for a while in the mill house, but in 1855 he bought property west of the stream in the village centre. It had been patented to John Dusenbury in 1807; today it is the site of a lovely Regency cottage. The land was owned from 1828 to 1853 by John Venton, and then for two years by John Dulmage before Booth acquired it. Since Regency was a popular style throughout most of that time, any of the men could have been the builder. Booth seems a

Regency cottage by the Mill Creek, Odessa

likely choice, however, since he had the necessary money. The site, by a mill stream, is ideal. The cottage is an imaginative combination of brick, stone quoins, wrought iron cresting, and wooden filigree – the latter on the railing of a verandah which surrounds the house.

Old directories record the vitality of the Booth family. In 1857, the *Kingston Directory* listed P.D. Booth's business in dry goods, groceries, and provisions, as well as J.R. Booth's potash factory and a Booth pot and tub factory. In 1865, the *Kingston Directory* recorded Booths of Odessa in the following occupations: agent, Odessa Woollen Mills; general merchant; proprietors of grist, saw, planing, and barley mills and of a cloth factory. The directories also refer to members of the Babcock family, who were well established in Odessa before they took over the Booth mills. The Babcocks were primarily wagon-makers, but were also general merchants, blacksmiths, and shoemakers.

A simple white frame house stands on the north side of the main street in the west end of Odessa. One of its early occupants was Thomas Depuis, who was listed in the *Kingston Directory* for 1865 as a physician and surgeon in Odessa. He probably built the house in the 1860s. The house can be identified by its stately door, with classical columns and many-paned side and transom windows. The present owners are descendants of Parker Smith Timmerman, Odessa's first postmaster and the man who was responsible for naming the town after a British engagement in the Crimean War.

Parker Timmerman married Mary Eleanor Booth, daughter of Benjamin and sister of the milling brothers. He operated a store on the main street and served as postmaster from 1841 to 1897. He also collected taxes for the school, distributed newspapers, acted as treasurer of Ernestown, wrote wills, and was active in church affairs.

The Timmerman store is one of a pair of well-preserved stone buildings on opposite corners of Main and Factory Streets on the south side of Main. Local histories refer to a revolutionary scheme devised by Timmerman which proves that genius sometimes lies in discovering the obvious. The mail was carried by stage coach along the York-Kingston road in large bags which contained all the letters for the scattered towns and villages along the route. When the mail coach arrived at Timmerman's post office, sometimes at night, he like his counterparts along the way had to go through the entire collection to find the local letters. He suggested that the mail be sorted once at the start and placed in small bags, one for each stop.

This inspiration was adopted, speeding mail delivery to a point which has probably not been surpassed since.

On the opposite corner from the scene of Timmerman's success is a companion building in stone, erected in 1840 and long a commercial building. It is now the Royal Bank, skilfully restored with a minimum of advertisement about its current function so that the original lines and fine windows are not unduly obscured. It is an example of what can be accomplished when businessmen and local historians work together to preserve a heritage for present use.

It is indicative of the confusion in spelling of surnames in the early 1800s that Christopher Fralick's name is spelled Fralic, Fraleigh, and Fralick on a single document – the title deed to land he received from the Crown in 1802. On the land (lot 4, concession 4, Ernestown) he built a home for his wife, Kathrine Smith, and in his will left her all the furnishings in the 'white house in which we live.' He stipulated in the will that she 'shall have command of the said house

Classical details in white frame, Main Street, Odessa

and garden as long as she remains my widow; she shall have a good milch cow kept for her during said term. If she chooses to trouble herself with said cow's milk, she shall be furnished with a sufficiency of flour, beef, vegetables, tea, sugar, pepper and alspice for her support during the said term and firewood for the fireplace and stove belonging to said house ... she shall also have nursing and proper attendance and decent burial after her decease.' One wonders why the whole of this bounty was dependent upon Kathrine's choosing to 'trouble herself with said cow's milk.' The farm itself was left to Christopher's son, John Lewis Fralick, who owned the house of which his mother had 'command.' Christopher's will also requested that John 'furnish my said wife with a saddle horse whenever she wants to ride to meeting or elsewhere.' The stone house which stands on the property today was built by John after his father's death in 1823. The kitchen was originally in the basement, and the long tail at the rear of the house grew with family needs.

Fralick Tavern, lot 28, concession 5, North Fredericksburgh

Near Napanee (lot 28, concession 5, North Fredericksburgh) is a frame house which commands notice today as it did when it was known as the Fralick Tavern, a popular coaching inn and meeting place. Its special character is due to a common but striking combination of narrow clapboard, original glass, a pillared verandah, and simple bargeboard. At one time a picket fence surrounded the house and gates and stiles stood at the driveway entrance. Just west of the former inn is one of the eighteen remaining milestones on the Napanee-Kingston road. The host of the inn was John Fralick. He acquired the land in 1809 from Ensign William Crawford and it remained in the family, passing later to Lydia Fralick Van Slyck.

William Herrington described the nearby hamlet of Morven in his *History of the County of Lennox and Addington* as a spot whose beginning and ending are hard to locate. It had, however, a lively past which is associated chiefly with taverns and politics. Morven was the only polling-place in the county for many years, he explained, and 'as the poll was held in one of the several wayside inns and the election lasted several days, and treating was considered quite the proper thing, and whiskey was cheap, it is very easy to conclude that it was to the interest of the tavern-keeper to remain on favourable terms with the party in power.' No doubt John Fralick and family received their full share of business during those marathon polling sessions.

5

Napanee-Deseronto

The framework of a mill rising in newly cleared land signified, as no trading post or log house could do, that a settlement had begun. The government had undertaken to transport and settle those loyal to the Crown, and their management of this huge undertaking had the backing of plans which can only be compared in detail with a military invasion. By 1785 it was apparent that the saw mill built in that year at Millhaven, and the saw and grist mills built the years before at Cataraqui, were not enough. Something had to be done for settlers who were a hard two days' travel to the west. Accordingly, in 1786 the government sent the man who had built the mills at Cataraqui to a site with good water power at Appanea Falls (later renamed Napanee). There Robert Clark established saw and grist mills as soon as the land was cleared. It would seem they were raised with equal amounts of rum and construction materials, judging by the accounts submitted:

March 23, 1786 – For raising the saw mill, 2 gallons and 3 pints of rum, 17 shillings 6 pence.
May 25. Four gallons and 1 quart of rum for raising the grist mill, 7 shillings 6 pence.
May 26. 1 quart of rum for the people at work in the water at the dam.

Around these mills grew the first settlement by the river. Its name, Clarkville, honoured Sergeant James Clark, government manager of the mills, not the millwright Robert Clark. James Clark was a government agent who had been with Governor Sir Frederick Haldimand in Quebec before coming to Appanea Falls. In 1789 he was posted to Fort Niagara.

By 1800 Hon. Richard Cartwright of Kingston had built another mill on the north side of the river. This signaled the beginning of a second settlement, a situation which for many years resulted in rival communities on either side of the Napanee River. Around 1812 the Clarkville mill was rented to Allan Macpherson, who became known as the 'laird' or 'king' of Napanee. Macpherson eventually owned a general store, a distillery, the mills, and a lumber business. In 1825 he built a frame house on the north side of the river at 180 Elizabeth Street, a site which would satisfy any laird.

The panelled front door symbolized the hospitality of the owner. The absence of a door handle on the exterior is typical of the period, when the door would be opened from within by the host. Originally the kitchen was in the basement and had a dirt floor, but in the 1830s a kitchen wing was added, on the east side, with servants' quarters above. The south side of the house, which faces the river, has an entrance door equal in grandeur to that on the north; over it is a beautiful window with side lights. The numerous windows, nine on each of the north and south faces, although aesthetically pleasing, must have presented real problems when it came to heating the large building. Macpherson House is now a museum, the scene of special entertainments conducted in the manner of the period in which it was built.

Allan Macpherson was the son of Lieutenant-Colonel Donald Macpherson of Laggan parish in Scotland, whose successful military career spanned forty-one years. His last position was in Kingston, where his 4th Loyal Veterans fortified the harbour. When Donald's wife Elspeth died, he married Ann Shaw, from the same part of Scotland, and in 1808 Allan joined his father and stepmother in Kingston. He brought with him his 'lines' – a letter of recommendation from his minister in Laggan, still in the family's possession: 'During his residence in his native parish he appeared to us to be a promising and well behaving young man, and as such is accordingly hereby recommended. [Signed] John Matheson, Minister.'

Allan moved to Napanee and in 1818 married Mary Fisher, the daughter of Judge Fisher of Adolphustown. Mary was the granddaughter of John and Mary Fisher of Killen in Scotland, whose 'lines' have also been preserved; they assure the reader that John and Mary behaved 'in their single and married state civilly, honestly and inoffensively and free of all public scandal.' Mary Macpherson came to be known in Napanee as 'Angel Mary,' a character trait which may have complemented her husband's nature. Although normally jovial, Allan could be stern in business dealings, in which he demanded integrity at all times.

'Angel Mary' was the recipient of an unusual bequest. In 1845 Frederick Hesford, of Richmond township in the Midland District, left her all his 'lands, tenements and hereditaments.' Her son, Donald, was an executor and her husband a witness, but the income from all Hesford's holdings was for her alone. To make this perfectly clear in the face of normal property arrangements of the time, he stipulated that the income was to be quite 'separate and apart from the control of her said husband for and during the term of her natural life.' After Mary's death, the estate was to go to her female children and their female heirs.

Allan Macpherson house, 180 Elizabeth Street, now a museum

The Macphersons were connected by marriage with the family of the first prime minister of Canada, Sir John A. Macdonald. Donald Macpherson's second wife, Ann Shaw, was the sister of John A. Macdonald's mother, and Donald welcomed Helen and Hugh Macdonald (John A.'s parents) when they came to Canada in 1820 and helped establish them in a house in Kingston. Later, young John found an outlet for his lively nature as a schoolboy in visits to the elder Macpherson's home. In 1832, when he was seventeen years old and already a lawyer, John moved to Napanee to operate a small branch office for his employer, George Mackenzie. During the year he spent there he found modest lodgings on the south side of the river, but spent much of his time in his second home, Allan Macpherson's spacious dwelling on Elizabeth Street. He thrived in the stimulating company and is said to have participated in skits for the entertainment of the family and their friends.

It is possible today to find three buildings in Clarkville (south Napanee) which are associated with John A. Macdonald's stay: 149 Hillside Avenue was called the Quakenbush Tavern, and was a meeting place he frequented; 369 William Street, now covered in green siding, was the Ramsay store presumably where he had his law office; 407 Huffman Street is thought to have been where he boarded. When a former resident at the last address removed a partition to make a larger room, he found legal papers bearing John A. Macdonald's signature.

Allan Macpherson moved from Napanee to Kingston in the mid-nineteenth century, and his son Donald took over his business and the house. Donald was not on the best of terms with his relative John A. Macdonald. He had followed the politician's advice in an investment, lost much money as a result, and never forgot it.

One of Napanee's more successful entrepreneurs, Alexander Campbell, chose a site for a large stone house on the south side of the river, on lot 15, concession 6, Fredericksburgh. Campbell was a surveyor by profession who became a merchant. His general store at Dundas and Centre Streets was a two-storey frame building. Its enclosed verandahs, according to Walter Herrington in *The History of the County of Lennox and Addington*, 'served as a shelter for some of the coarser wares exposed for sale and as an excellent loafing place where the idle used to congregate to gossip or wile away

Alexander Campbell's home, lot 15, concession 6, Fredericksburgh

the hours of waiting for the stage-coach with the mail.' Campbell also built the Campbell House hotel, acted as postmaster, and owned the Napanee *Standard*. His home reflects his success. He purchased the property in 1844 for £300 from James Armstrong.

The site was called Campbell's Rocks, and on this solid base Alexander built the house of stone quarried from the Napanee River at its front. Originally, a verandah enclosed the east half of the front of the house and the east side. In his prosperity, Campbell had a deer park in the forested part of the property. But in 1863 he died, and within three years a mortgage on the house was foreclosed and the land passed out of Campbell hands.

Campbell seemed to be a frequent topic of discussion. Public opinion was strongly for or against him, as in these excerpts from a newspaper called *The Bantling*:

19 March 1859: Last week there was a petition in circulation to take the Post Office from Alex Campbell, Esq.; but we believe the signers were scarce and the petition and its originators 'up a stump' – the least we can do is hope so.

25 June 1859: Our contemporary says – 'the two gentlemen (???) who have lately made a practice of entering the lobby of the Post Office, and abusing the Postmaster when alone, and making up mails, will please bear in mind, that on repetition of such conduct, they will be brought before the proper tribunal for the offence.'

We wonder who the eccentric GENTLEMEN could be.

East of the Campbell house, at 10 Alfred Street, south Napanee, is the Briggs house. It is a fine substantial stone structure with thick walls, simple hand-carved woodwork in the interior, and wide pine floors in beautiful condition today. Large parlour and dining rooms are located on the main floor, each with a fireplace. On the second floor, a wide hall opens to ample bedrooms.

It is difficult to date the building exactly. The property, an original Crown grant to James McKenzie, was purchased by Thomas Briggs in 1849. Thomas sold a portion of the land to his son James in 1856, and by 1869 a plan of south Napanee showed the house in what was then called the Briggs subdivision. There is not a great deal known about the Briggs family either. James Briggs is described, in an 1878 county atlas, as a retired merchant who had come to Canada from England in 1825 – presumably with his parents. The 1851 census found Thomas Briggs, then aged seventy-two, living in a log house with his wife Sarah. Since the stone house appears on the 1869 plan, it must have been built either by Thomas when he was in his seventies or eighties or, more likely, by James. It is of interest to note that the 1851 census-taker described Sarah, then sixty-three, by occupation as 'labourer' – an apt description of the role of the woman of the house at the time.

Napanee has three imposing public buildings of early date. All were built following changes in the status of the town.

The incorporation of Napanee in 1855 immediately sparked interest in the building of a town hall. Council approved the plan and at the same time approved the purchase of a fire engine for the safety of the community, which had more than a thousand residents. The proposed outlay of public funds for these two projects resulted in much debate about their relative merits. One citizen wrote to the

Briggs house, 10 Alfred Street, south Napanee

editor of the Napanee *Reformer* in August 1855 that the 'municipality is too poor ... to warrant us in spending money for the sake of ornament and show. That we require a Fire-Engine I think no-one will deny but that we need a Market House which will cost £1,000 or thereabouts some may be inclined to doubt.' The brick market building and town hall was built, however, and is located at 124 John Street. John A. Macdonald is reputed to have spoken from a balcony over its doorway. The original roofed stalls along the sides have gone and a portico has been added. This 'useless ornament' is still a handsome structure and has weathered well over 120 years.

In 1863 the County of Lennox and Addington was separated from Frontenac County and Napanee became the county town. This prompted the construction of two other important buildings – the county court house and the jail. The architect was John Power and the builder John Forin, whose tender of $33,146 covered both buildings. They were completed by 1864. The court house stands at 91

Napanee Town Hall

Thomas Street East and the jail, now the Lennox and Addington Museum is directly behind it. Both buildings are stone. The court house, with its impressive arched portico, is surmounted by a finely detailed cupola. The old court room is on the second floor.

Old jail records have been preserved, and a retired judge has uncovered many details, among which are the following: of those housed in the jail between 1865 and 1874, ninety-seven were Irish, forty-two English, twenty-nine American, seven Scottish, and one came from elsewhere; in 1861 the jail rules required prisoners to bathe and keep hair and beards short; in 1878 prisoners doing extra-mural labour were given a breakfst of one pint of oat meal or Indian corn meal, eight ounces of bread, and one pint of pea coffee sweetened with molasses.

The house at 138 Robinson Street was built for a man who was called in his obituary 'a veritable encyclopedia on matters Political.' John Stevenson was elected the first Speaker of the Legislative

Lennox and Addington County Court House

Assembly of Ontario in 1867. Another successful local entrepreneur, like Allan Macpherson and Alexander Campbell he had a multitude of business interests. He had been born in 1812 in New Jersey, but came to Canada with his parents and attended school in Brockville. He later taught near Maitland. From 1831 to 1850 he worked in general stores, first as an apprentice and later as owner of his own shop. When he located in Napanee he had interests in lumbering, milling, general contracting, and general merchandising. His will spoke of other involvements, including a piano factory at Kingston and a brush factory at Napanee.

In 1869 Stevenson purchased what became known as the Stevenson Block from John Solomon Cartwright, a Kingston lawyer. That same year he took out a mortgage of $2,875 to build his large brick home. The site still has some of the large pines which at one time covered the district. A full verandah at the main entrance has been removed. Heavy brackets under the eaves are typical of those found on many buildings of the late nineteenth century in west Napanee. Indeed, on some neighbouring houses the woodwork is much more elaborate than on the Stevenson house. The Victorian homes in this hill area have given Napanee a reputation as a beautiful residential town. The west end was separated from the early town site by a large marshy area, so that it was not considered suitable for settlement in the early 1800s: hence the lesser age of its dwellings.

Ira Kimmerly was a merchant and trader. At one point (the letter in the county museum is undated), he wrote to the mayor and council tendering 'to collect market tolls and act as Market Clerk and see that the market ground is kept clear etc. for the sum of four hundred dollars per year.' In 1867 he purchased the land at what is now 208 Dundas Street West and probably began construction of his Victorian gothic house, as mortgages were taken out in that year and in 1874. A steep peaked gable with delicate bargeboard is located over its central door and ornate porch. He used good materials and skilled craftsmen, for the house is in excellent condition more than a century after its construction.

It is difficult to determine the first owner and builder of the board-on-board house at 131 West Street. The land was part of the large J.S. Cartwright holdings until 1852, when it was sold to George Bowers. It is possible that Bowers built the house since he held the land for eleven years, at which point it passed to his wife Mary. Or it could have been built by Edwin Mallory, who bought the

John Stevenson house, 138 Robinson Street

property in 1867. The house is shown on an 1873 map of Napanee.
Whichever owner was responsible, he was a man with tastes in construction unique to the area. The windows have been altered and the
transom over the front door is gone.

The road between Napanee and Kingston was the first in Upper
Canada to be macadamized – raised above the surrounding ground
and finished with a layer of graded stones. It was built between 1837
and 1839. This was also the only section of the York-to-Kingston
Road that was measured and marked by milestones. Eighteen of the
original stones remain, but mystery surrounds their origin: who put
them there, and why? Two possible answers are both connected
with the Cartwright family. The first, part of a family legend, is the
more dramatic. The second, much less adventurous, is probably the
real one.

As a young man, Richard Cartwright of Kingston (a grandson of
the pioneer Hon. Richard Cartwright, and a future bank president,

Ira Kimmerly house, 208 Dundas Street West

cabinet minister, and knight) made regular trips to Napanee. There he collected the quarterly rents from the family mills. On one occasion, when he was leaving for home with more than $2,000 on his person, he was met by a group of highwaymen. He was a fine horseman and outrode the robbers; but ever after he took a different route each time he left Napanee to go east – riding through farms and across fences before returning eventually to the main road. The difficulty was that he could never determine exactly where he was when he rejoined the highway. His answer, one story goes, was to instal the milestones.

The other story credits the stones to John Solomon Cartwright, Sir Richard's uncle. John Solomon, a member of the Legislature, was instrumental in the plans to macadamize the Napanee to Kingston road and probably suggested the milestones at that time.

Deseronto received its name from Captain John Deseryonteo, a Mohawk chief who is credited with directing his band to the land in

Board on board with belvedere, 131 West Street

Upper Canada they had earned as Loyalists. The government awarded the Indians property on the Bay of Quinte and at Brantford, but portions of this were later sold. The Quinte land was named Tyendinaga Township, after the Indian name of the Mohawk chief whom the English called Joseph Brant. Thayendanegea means 'tied together,' like a bundle of sticks.

A simple wooden church was erected in Tyendinaga Township just after 1786 to serve the many converts to Christianity. When its fabric deteriorated, some of the Indian land was sold to finance a new stone building, Christ Church, Tyendinaga, completed in 1843. It still stands near Deseronto and bears a strong resemblance to two other churches – St John's, York Mills, in northern Toronto, and Christ Church, Holland Landing – designed by the same architect, John Howard. All have similar three-sectioned towers and similar placement of windows. Initially, here, a spire reached 107 feet into the air, but it was destroyed by lightning.

One name looms larger than any other in the history of Deseronto. During the last half of the nineteenth century, the Rathbun Company was known throughout the country as part of a vast financial empire that started with lumbering and grew to include railroad interests, cement works, a fleet of vessels, a shipyard, a printing business, and sash and door manufacturing. Many of the ornate mouldings and brackets seen today on Napanee's fine Victorian homes came from Rathbun's.

This success story started with an American, Hugo Burghardt Rathbun, who received title to most of the Deseronto town site in 1846. He built a sawmill and opened a general store. Eight years later, Rathbun's young son, Edward Wilkes, arrived to help. He was only fourteen years old at the time, but in less than six years the entire management of H.B. Rathbun & Company was turned over to him. When the firm received a federal charter twenty-two years later, its assets had grown to two million dollars.

Edward W. Rathbun was a Canadian version of a Horatio Alger hero. Of humble birth and with little education, he became, by virtue of hard work and imagination, a rich and powerful man. He had a social conscience as well: he was a benefactor of Queen's University and governor of the Kingston School of Mines, forerunner of the Queen's Engineering Faculty. As a devout Christian, he acted as superintendent of the Presbyterian Sunday School in Deseronto for forty-two years. He put his beliefs into practice by donating land for all the churches in the town.

Rathbun built his impressive frame house at 313 Dundas Street, overlooking the town. Here he entertained many prominent guests, among them the prime minister, Sir John A. Macdonald. After the death of his first wife, Elizabeth Burt, he married a Toronto woman, Bunella McMurrich. He was admired and respected by the citizens of the town he 'owned.' One biographer recorded the scene when Edward brought his ailing father home to Deseronto in 1884 after a winter in the western United States. The two men were met at the railway station by more than one thousand people, the municipal council, and the town band. Their carriages were pulled home through the streets – not by horses, but by fifty citizens. Edward died in 1903.

The Presbyterian Church of the Redeemer in Deseronto has a history that goes back to an ecumenical white clapboard building

Edward Wilkes Rathbun house, 313 Dundas Street, Deseronto

which served the Anglicans in the morning, the Methodists in the afternoon, and the Presbyterians in the evening. In 1881, work began on the stone Presbyterian church which serves the community today. The church was built and furnished as a gift to the town by Hugo B. Rathbun.

6

Belleville

In most cases the communities along the York-Kingston Road had one or two names before the present official one was adopted. Often these names are, in themselves, clues to the history of the area. Such is the case at Belleville, which was known until 1816 as Meyers' Creek.

The man who built the first grist mill in the area and gave his name to the settlement was Captain John Walden Meyers, a Loyalist of German descent who was one of the most famous scouts in the Revolutionary War. Born in New York State in 1745, he had been christened Hans Waltermeyer. As a young man he married Polly Kruger and took up tenant farming near Albany. When the Revolution broke out he was reluctant to support either side, since the livelihood of his family was totally dependent upon his working the farm. But as persecutions became common, and he saw a neighbour being tarred, feathered, and hanged, he could no longer remain neutral. He opted for the Crown. His parents sympathized with the rebels, and this may have been the reason for his change of nàme.

Once his decision was made, life changed dramatically. Meyers scouted for recruits, took prisoners, conducted secret raids, and reported rebel movements. He frequently crossed rebel territory carrying messages from one army outpost to another. It wasn't long before the Meyers farm was taken over by rebels, but Polly and the seven children escaped to the British area of New York on Long Island.

Meyers' most famous raid was the attempted kidnapping of an

American general, Philip Schuyler, from his home in Albany. Many stories have been told of this unsuccessful venture – one suggests that the general hid under a cask on which the children's nanny sat. It has been reported too that some of Meyers' men stole Schuyler's silver but that Meyers later insisted that it be returned to the general. Possibly Ann Schuyler (whose adventures are recorded in the Colborne chapter) was in the house at the time of the raid.

Meyers became notorious, and it is remarkable that he escaped capture for his appearance was as memorable as his exploits – he was a big man, with fiery red hair. Yet he always managed to evade the parties sent to find him. After the war, he and his family settled in Thurlow, after brief stays at Missisquoi Bay, Ernestown, and Sidney. There they built one of the first brick houses in Upper Canada, a large two-storey Georgian structure on a hill overlooking the Moira River. It was referred to locally as Meyers' Castle. In it he entertained distinguished guests such as John Strachan and many customers from the nearby mills.

Besides operating the saw and grist mills, Meyers ran a store, owned boats which transported supplies for local settlers, bought furs, made whiskey and cider, and lent money. At his death, much of his £12,000 estate was in notes from settlers. He left everything to his grandchildren 'males and phemales share and share alike.' To his second wife Sophia, whom he married after Polly's death, he left 'one half of the dwelling house which I now live in, namely the south west half, and half of the hall, the half of the cellar and also half of the kitchen.'

Two buildings remain in Belleville that are directly associated with the Meyers family. The first is a house built by George Bleecker, a son of John Walden Meyers' daughter Catherine and her husband 'Squire' John Bleecker. This frame house, at 260 Dundas Street East, is on part of Meyers' crown grant and stands near the spot where he camped when he first came to the area. The earliest part was built in the 1820s and forms the middle section of the present building. It was the first home of George and his wife, Elsie Ritchie. In the 1840s they added the two fine rooms which form the front section today and, at the same time, built a verandah that surrounded the house on three sides. Only the front portion of the verandah remains. The gabled rear portion of the house was a later addition.

George Bleecker had a brother, Tobias, and it was in all probability his son-in-law, Ellis Burrell, who built the simple stone building that stands by the river near Station Street. Construction details suggest that the building was a product of the 1860s or '70s. For many years it was part of Burrell's Axe Factory, a thriving enterprise that shipped its products as far as the United Kingdom. In 1878, the Montreal *Commercial Review* referred to the business as 'the Leading and most extensive work of this kind in the Dominion.'

Not far to the west of George Bleecker's house is a single-storey stone building (109 Dundas Street East). It was the home of John Way Maybee and his wife, Martha McArthur. In his preparatory notes for *A History of the Early Settlement of Upper Canada*, Dr Canniff related that 'J.W. Maybee of Belleville came to Canada with his father in 1793, when he was about 14 years old. His grandfather was a German, grandmother Dutch, his mother was English, by name Way. His father was an American Revolutionary soldier. They settled near Picton.' Maybee purchased his property in 1833

Home of George Bleecker, 260 Dundas Street East

and built his house shortly thereafter. Much of what is known about early life in Belleville comes from his wife's recollections, which are among the Canniff papers in the Ontario Archives. Martha once named the people living in houses within the original town limits in 1809 as 'McIntosh, Johnson, Dr Spareham, Major Thompson, P. Holmes, Mrs Simpson (who owned the tavern), R. Leavens, Simmons (a cooper), S. McNabb, Ames, Ackerman, Stewart and Maybee.' She recalled seeing, as a girl of five, the construction scaffolding still standing at the Meyers house on the outskirts of the town.

Next door to the Maybee house, at 103 Dundas Street East, is Montrose Cottage, once the home of George Henderson. He bought the property in 1849 and a short time later built the handsome brick house with its four pilasters. Henderson had a busy law practice and, in 1854, served as defence counsel in a notable murder case. The accused, from Tyendinaga Township, was a squatter who had re-

Burrell's Axe Factory, by the Moira River

fused to leave the land on which he had settled and, when a new owner came to take possession, shot and killed him. Henderson was unsuccessful that time, and the case ended in Belleville's first hanging. He acted more successfully at various times as crown attorney, was elected alderman, and served as mayor of Belleville in 1874.

Several substantial frame houses were erected along South Front Street during the 1820s. Most have been greatly altered, but it was probably these buildings to which Susanna Moodie referred when she later wrote: 'The dwellings of the wealthier portion of the community [Belleville] were distinguished by a coat of white or yellow paint, with green or brown doors and window blinds [shutters]; while the houses of the poorer class retained the dull grey which the plain boards always assume after a short exposure to the weather.'

One house, at 75 South Front Street, remains relatively untouched. It was the home of John Thompson, one of the many early settlers who, with distinguished military careers behind them, stayed and became merchants. Mrs Maybee said that Thompson was in Belleville in 1809. During the War of 1812 he served as a captain (later major) in the local militia. By 1820 he had received a Crown grant, and his pleasant frame house was likely built shortly afterward.

Thompson's neighbour to the south was Captain John McIntosh. He too served in the militia, and was a business associate of John Walden Meyers. In 1815, McIntosh drowned in the Bay of Quinte while attempting to swim ashore from a becalmed boat. His widow later built the house at 45 South Front Street, but its original frame structure is concealed behind the present façade.

Not long after the house at 43 Bridge Street West was built, its owner came to an untimely end. His name was James McNabb, and he was impaled on a bayonet – Belleville's only casualty in the Rebellion of 1837. This fatality occurred during a disorganized alarm in a local hotel when, in the darkness, McNabb ran into a weapon held by one of his own men.

James was the grandson of Dr James McNabb, a Loyalist surgeon from Vermont who had served in the Revolutionary War under General Burgoyne. Dr McNabb died in 1780 but his four sons, James, Simon, Alexander, and Colin, all came to Upper Canada a few years later. The first two eventually settled at Belleville, James on the outskirts of the village. During the War of 1812 he housed members of the militia in his home, and had a run-in with John

Walden Meyers which resulted in a life-long feud between them. It began when McNabb accused Meyers of high treason for allegedly refusing to provide food, lodging, and horses for the troops and of 'taking his pleasure sleigh to pieces and concealing it in his garret ... in order to render it useless to His Majesty's service.' (The quotation comes from a 'register of persons connected with high treason during the War of 1812–14' in the Ontario Archives.) Meyers countered by accusing McNabb of charging excessively for his services. He also held McNabb responsible for an incident in which billeted soldiers fought in his house: both Meyers and his wife were injured in the ruckus – he was cut on the head with a sabre – and she never recovered.

James McNabb became an MLA in 1808 and in 1816 was involved in having the town's name changed from Meyers' Creek to Bellville (the original spelling). In that year, the lieutenant-governor of Upper Canada and his wife, Lady Bella Gore, stopped at Mrs Simpson's tavern en route from Kingston to York. Messengers were sent throughout the area to announce a ball in their honour. Uniforms were brought out and the occasion was a colourful success. After the visit the town adopted the name of Bellville in honour of Lady Gore.

McNabb, it would appear, was not universally admired. He was described by a political opponent (according to Gerald Boyce in *Historic Hastings*) as 'a mean malignant man' who had treated the complainant to several drinks at a local tavern 'in order to loosen his tongue and make him say something seditious.'

James McNabb died in 1820. Twelve years later, his son purchased land on Bridge Street and built the two-storey stone structure which began this family history. In 1859 the house was bought by a lawyer, Horace Yeomans, a descendant of Loyalist settlers who came to the Belleville area in the 1780s. It was he who added the gables and the elaborate, two-storey verandah with its ornate treillage – a modification that earned the house its nickname, The Riverboat.

Just below The Riverboat, at 190 James Street, is a small house built by Henry Hagerman, the grandson of a Loyalist who emigrated from New York State. The land was part of the pioneer James McNabb's extensive holdings in the area around his house; Hagerman bought it when McNabb subdivided the property, and held it until 1852. At some point during those seventeen years he built the handsome classical revival house, with its gable end facing the street. Three of the four original columns still support the gallery.

John Wedderburne Dunbar Moodie and his wife Susanna came to Belleville in 1840. Two years later they purchased the stone cottage at 114 Bridge Street West and settled down to enjoy life in this busy town. The house had been built in the 1830s by George and Hannah Cowper, without its present dormers and portico. Before moving to Belleville the Moodies had spent seven years on a farm near Peterborough, but had come to recognize that, like many English settlers of the gentle classes, they were totally unequipped for wilderness farming: much as they were prepared to work hard, they lacked the skills it needed. In her book, *Roughing It in the Bush*, Susanna described the constant struggle with the land, the harsh climate, frequent illnesses, and loneliness.

When John Moodie was appointed first sheriff of the Victoria District, the family moved to Belleville with pleasure. It was at this

The Riverboat, 43 Bridge Street West

point that Susanna wrote *Roughing It in the Bush* and later, *Life in the Clearings*. She contributed articles to many magazines as well. In her writings she admitted their failure as settlers and cautioned those about to embark on a similar life to face reality rather than to view wilderness living through a romantic haze. She loved her Belleville house. 'There stood my peaceful, happy home,' she later recalled, 'the haven of rest to which Providence had conducted me after the storms and trials of many years.' As a writer, she was a curiosity to the local people. She remarked that some of the ladies were 'amazed' to find that she looked like everyone else. One woman asked many personal questions about Susanna's age, teeth, and health and finally concluded that the writer was 'but a humly body after all.'

The Moodies had seven children, the third child and first son being John A. Dunbar Moodie. The house across from the Moodies', at 110 Bridge Street West, was sold in 1866 to Alexander D. Moodie – pro-

Classical revival at 190 James Street

bably that elder son.

Sheriff Moodie died in 1869. After his death Susanna moved to Toronto to live with a married daughter. She died in 1885 and is buried in Belleville.

Life was far from easy for the women who lived in Upper Canada, and their mortality rate was high. Time and time again, the records of early families show that many men had several wives, sometimes as many as four or five in succession. Women died from having too many babies, from lack of adequate medical care, and from overwork. Often it was a combination of all these factors. The story of one such woman is graphically told by the three gravestones standing behind a house at 208 John Street.

This house, known as The Lodge, was the home of Daniel Ackerill, an English farrier (blacksmith and horse doctor) who came to Canada in 1832. Eleven years later he married. Under the first small gravestone lies a daughter, Delia – she died in 1846. Under the sec-

Home of Susanna and John Moodie, 114 Bridge Street West

ond stone is a son, James Henry: he died the following year. The third stone marks the joint grave of 'Mary Ann, wife of Daniel and infant daughter.' They died in 1848. Mary Ann was eighteen years old.

By the time of the 1851 census, Daniel Ackerill had remarried, another Mary Ann. In 1861 his second wife had a son, Daniel Henry, who became one of the first students to attend the Ontario Veterinary College: his veterinary practise eventually extended from Oshawa to Brockville and his horse and cattle remedies – Ackerill's All-Round Liniment, and Ackerill's Powders – were well known throughout the district.

Daniel and Mary Ann built their splendid brick house in 1844. (It appears on an 1845 map.) Daniel was a member of the Loyal Orange Lodge (Royal Scarlet Chapter), and built the second storey of his house with added height so that the chapter could meet comfortably

The Lodge, home of Daniel Ackerill and meeting place of the Loyal Orange Lodge, 208 John Street

there. The high arch at the front of the house on the second level indicates the location of the meeting room. In 1847 and 1869, he sold pieces of his property to the Lodge so that it could extend its quarters. The trustees acting for the Orange Order in 1869 were Ramsay Dougall, Peter Post, and one of Belleville's gifts to posterity – Mackenzie Bowell, the future prime minister of Canada. For many years the Orange Lodge occupied the Ackerill house and played its part in a religious conflict that was never very far from the surface in that part of the world. Today the house is being carefully and authentically restored by its owner who, ironically, happens to be a Roman Catholic.

In March 1855, Delia Buell O'Hare wrote to her father saying, 'you have done a very great deal for my comfort and happiness in getting me a nice place to live in.' Delia was referring to her prospective home, a handsome brick house at 231 John Street, not far from the Ackerills. Its land was part of a large Crown grant to John Taylor in 1804. Forty-four years later the property was sold to James Ross who, in turn, sold it to John Jordon in 1853. One of these two men built the house that Andrew Buell bought for his daughter and her husband, John O'Hare.

The prolific correspondence of Andrew Buell has been preserved in the Ontario Archives so it is possible, through letters exchanged between him and the O'Hares, to learn much of their life and the problems they faced there. Delia described the house to her father in a letter dated 3 March 1855:

I was up to take the measure of the sitting room as Mr Jordon told John he was willing to move anytime. When I asked Mrs Jordon what day she would commence to move she said they would have trouble getting her out. I think the house can be made very comfortable, the rooms are very small but there are plenty of them and in the summer some of the partitions can be taken down and made more to my taste. The kitchen is a nice one and there is a pantry off it with a sink and soft water pump which pleased me more than the rest of the house. Upstairs there is a nice hall, by placing a large stove in it all the bedrooms may be warmed nicely.

Delia had been in poor health and her husband wrote of his concern to her father:

She ... has the toothache and sometimes the earache ... it keeps her up most of the night ... she has weakness and want of circulation in the extremities ... she is too weak to walk very much ... I am going to buy her a nice quiet horse.

Two days before that letter, Delia had written to her father of her worry about John. He had, it seems, felt ill and was 'drinking heavily apparently at the advice of a doctor who told him that "gin was the only thing that he could prescribe".'

In January 1855, John O'Hare wrote to his father-in-law:

You have of course heard ... of my election as Mayor of Belleville ... The Orange party and the Methodists are much annoyed at having a Papist Mayor and some of my liberal friends express their disappointment also! The hostility to Catholics is indeed deeply rooted in most Protestant minds ... They think a Catholic can't do his duty as he might: so far as I am concerned they are mistaken for I would punish Catholics when wrong just as I would a Protestant and perhaps more severely.

Home of John and Delia Buell O'Hare, 231 John Street

(The antagonism between Catholics and Protestants seemed particularly strong at this time. In 1860, it caused the cancellation of a Royal visit to Belleville. The Prince of Wales, the future Edward VII, was touring Canada, and the Orange Lodge had erected numerous banners and flags celebrating their Order. The Royal yacht anchored in Belleville harbour but the prince refused to disembark. He had previously objected to religious and political displays, and on this occasion he simply went on his way.)

Delia's father, Andrew Buell, was a prominent lawyer and a friend and confidant of William Lyon Mackenzie – even when the latter was in exile after his unsuccessful rebellion. For a man of influence actively engaged in business, he enjoyed an unusual hobby on his visits to Belleville. He, his daughter, and other residents of the town belonged to a group that met to participate in spirit rapping. On one of Buell's visits, he and Delia were successful in reaching the deceased Mrs Buell in the 'spirit world.' Buell made notes about the evening and expressed in them a feeling that his wife had not undergone any change of personality since her death. 'Being of a sanguine and warm temperament,' he wrote, 'and having clear ideas of her own, she was inclined to show impatience and derision when not readily understood.' Her rappings in reply to her husband's questions were just as explosive as her responses had been when she was alive.

The house at 184 William Street is an example of Victorian gothic carpentry at its most creative – a flourish of sculptured wood that is lavish but stops short of excess. It is the work of James Noseworthy, a local builder. The house was built for the Wallbridges, and if it were not important for its architecture, it would be so for its connection with this early Belleville family.

When Elijah Wallbridge came from the United States to Canada in 1800, he bought two thousand acres of land in Ameliasburgh, and gave each of his five sons a three-hundred acre farm. One of the sons, William, later purchased a large tract of land in what would become Belleville, including the William Street property. He and his wife, Mary Everett, also purchased the White House, one of the first buildings in what was then Meyers' Creek – a frame house at Front and Dundas Streets that had been owned by Mrs Simpson, proprietor of Simpson's Tavern. It became the Wallbridges' home and later that of their son, Hon. Lewis Wallbridge, who became Speaker of the Legislative Assembly of the United Canadas in the days just preceding Confederation.

In 1855 a mortgage was taken out on the William Street property, presumably to finance construction of the present building. For some years the house was occupied by Adam Henry Wallbridge, until, after the death of his wife, he moved to the White House to live with his brother Lewis, with whom he practised law. The house on William Street stayed in the family until 1921. It remains in excellent condition. The White House, one of the most important early buildings in Belleville was demolished in 1973.

At the western end of Belleville are three houses built quite early in the last century. The oldest part of the stone house at 153 Dundas Street West was erected by John Chisholm, of whom little is known except that he served as an officer during the War of 1812. The Crown granted him two hundred acres in 1798 and he probably built his house shortly after that date. In 1817, all his property was sold to Philip Zwick, a Loyalist.

Zwick had arrived in Canada shortly after the Revolutionary

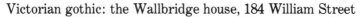

Victorian gothic: the Wallbridge house, 184 William Street

War with his wife Elizabeth, and for a time settled in Fredericks-burgh. Early records show that their son Charles was born there in 1789. They soon moved to Meyers' Creek, however, for the baptis-mal records there list 'Philip, son of Filip and Elizabet Zwick, Bap-tized Thurlow [Township], March 3, 1796.' It is not certain where the Zwick family lived when they first came to the district but they knew John Chisholm as early as 1795. This is made clear in a will written that year by David Vanderhider, leaving to 'my beloved friend Phillip Sweek all the following articles vist. one broad axe, one brass kettle and one iron pott.' He also left Zwick the payment for 35 bushels of potatoes and two bushels of wheat bought from John Chisholm.

The Canniff papers in the Ontario Archives provided additional glimpses into life in this pioneer community, and in them the Zwick name appears occasionally. In 1817 Philip was serving as a lieute-nant in the militia and in this capacity was a member of a court martial. John Henesy, the defendant, was accused of refusing to toast the King. Henesy protested that he couldn't see why he should have to say 'God bless,' to a man who did not give him more than six pence a day. He was found guilty and fined one pound and costs.

In the following year, one of Zwick's sons, Philip Jr, was charged with assaulting a local woman but was discharged. The explanation is written on the back of the warrant sworn out for his arrest: 'Philip Swick, Junior, proves that Mary Stimers on this affair was the first aggressor, and pelted him with stones at the time the within affray took place, and that it was after that he struck her with a whip.'

Philip Zwick lived on Dundas Street until his death in 1833. The house was left to another son, George. Sometime in mid-century it was gutted by fire and the present stone cottage was built around the remaining stone walls. Like the original, this is a 'bank house,' built snugly into the side of the hill with access at the rear to the kitchen and sitting room on the lower level. The front door is on the upper level. The house overlooks the Bay of Quinte and Zwick's Island on the south.

John Chisholm's cousin Alexander lived a short distance to the west. The house he built, so like those in his native Scotland, still stands at 317 Dundas Street West. It is one of the oldest houses in this part of Ontario and, although it has been altered during the years, it is still in remarkably good condition.

It is difficult to date exactly. Chisholm's name does not appear on the title until 1809 but he likely built the house before then. The year 1805 appears above the bake oven. Possibly the house was built even earlier, for Chisholm was a middle-aged man at the turn of the century and he and his wife had ten children, making a substantial house such as this almost a necessity.

Chisholm had emigrated to North America in 1775, stayed for a few months near Albany, New York, but left there in September of that year 'finding it inconvenient to live in the Country' – due, no doubt, to the unsettling political situation. He spent the following winter in Quebec, serving with the British militia. After the war he eventually settled on the north shore of the Bay of Quinte, near his brother Archibald and his cousin John. Not surprisingly, his house has undergone many changes since it was built. A larger door has replaced the original, and the shutters are obviously a recent addition. Inside, the steep and narrow stairs to the second floor were removed and replaced with a wider and less hazardous staircase.

Alexander Chisholm house, 317 Dundas Street West

The low, beamed ceiling and the massive fireplace remain, however, and help retain the atmosphere of an earlier day.

William Hutton was a gentleman farmer from Ireland who settled on land just west of Belleville, now 250 Dundas Street West. Before deciding that Hastings County offered the best available land, he travelled through much of Upper Canada studying agricultural opportunities and getting to know the country. In letters to his family at home, he described Canada as it appeared to a newcomer in the 1830s. Much of what he saw shocked him. In a letter to his mother, he remarked on 'the depravity of the young people generally – cursing, swearing and drinking and passing their time in lewd conversation and gossip, not appearing to have the least wish to improve their minds ... Smoking, drinking and blaspheming are the order of the day. In Belleville, I have not heard so much of the latter – but the smoking, drinking and spitting are abominable, and not the least offensive is the chewing of tobacco which prevails greatly.'

Once he had bought his farm, Hutton was anxious to have his wife and five children join him. His letters home paint a rosier picture of the new country:

I will not raise your hopes about it, but it entirely pleases me – fine soil, beautiful situation, close to one of the best markets in Canada, and a most healthy climate. There has been no case of fever and ague since 1829. It slopes beautifully down to the edge of the bay, and of course water is plentiful, a great consideration.'

Later in his letter, Hutton told his wife that the country was becoming civilized for

The children as well as ladies are most beautifully dressed in silks with their veils and parasols. Do not have the idea that anything will do for Canada. It is quite a country. It will be too gay for you. The ladies are princesses in their dress, but I don't think much of their minds from what I have seen.

Sensing that his wife might have a few misgivings about the move, he added:

It is absolutely essential to my happiness that there should be contentment, and not the symptom of a complaint, and I am quite sure, knowing such to be the case, that you will train your mind in that spirit. If you feel that you cannot be happy at such a distance from home, I would say certainly remain until you can train your mind to it, and send the children forward, but I have a full confidence in you that your love for me is not that of a day or an hour, but that you will feel henceforth such pure affection for me that you will endeavour to sooth the sorrows which a separation from a beloved country and beloved friends naturally produces in a warm heart. Need I say that my affection will continue unchanged, and that I shall endeavour to sooth the sorrows of your still warmer heart? I need not say it; you know that I love you.

Fanny Hutton and their five children arrived in New York in September 1834. Although her husband had assured her, 'you will think nothing of the voyage; you will wonder what excuse you had for contemplating it with such horror,' the trip was in fact terrify-

Home of William and Fanny Hutton, 250 Dundas Street West

ing. The crossing took forty-four days, during which two of the children contracted typhus and were so ill that they were unable to continue on to Upper Canada for several weeks.

The family eventually reached Belleville and settled in their new home, Sidney Cottage, before Christmas 1834. They lived there for many years, working long hours on the farm. Hutton supplemented their income by teaching, but it was a long time before Fanny wore silk or veil or carried a parasol. The story of their life is told in Hutton's letters to his mother, which he continued to write until his death in 1861. They have been published in a book by Gerald Boyce, *Hutton of Hastings*.

Sidney Cottage was already on the farm when Hutton purchased it in 1834. It had been built for Seth Meacham, a pioneer doctor who came to Upper Canada in 1801. For many years he was the only doctor between Kingston and Cobourg. After the Huttons bought the house, several additions and improvements were made. The front part, originally frame, was covered with fieldstone from the farm, and a connecting section was built between it and a stone building at the rear. In 1859 a verandah was built surrounding the front part on three sides, and later a tower was added over the front door. Today, the verandah has gone but the tower remains, giving the house an unusual but not unpleasant appearance. Inside, an imposing staircase leads up to this tower and two adjacent small rooms. It seems likely that at one time an opening at the landing led to the centre portion of the house: this would explain so splendid a staircase – much too grand to lead only to the little tower room.

Hutton left the house to his wife and their invalid daughter Frances, but added in his will: 'I do hereby expressly recommend and enjoin my dear wife and my dear daughter Frances, that if at any time during their lives ... any one or more of my other children should require a home (they being unmarried or widowed) [they] ... will offer and allow [them] to live at my said dwelling house and remain with them so long as they or she may require it.'

7

Trenton

The River Trent was the symbol of Port Trent's prosperity. It flowed swiftly down to the bay, brim full of lumber moving with the spring floods. The vast pine forests to the north supplied logs for the first mills of the Hawley lumber business, founded in 1814, and in later years for the giant Gilmour Lumber enterprises. The industry brought settlers, lumbermen, and entrepreneurs to the area. But they did not come until well after 1800, and after adjacent areas were established. The reason was, again, the river. The swampy land on either side of it discouraged growth. Later the river split Port Trent firmly down the middle, inhibiting communication and travel between the two fledgling communities on its banks. In the 1830s a permanent bridge was finally built, and the town began to grow.

Before that, travellers had to cross the river by a ferry. For many years it was operated by 'Squire' John Bleecker, son-in-law of Belleville's John Walden Meyers, and one of the many Loyalists who achieved legendary (even if sometimes mythical) status. Bleecker had joined Jessup's Rangers as a youth of fifteen, and later had settled near Kingston with his family. After marrying Catherine Meyers, he had first located at Carrying Place, working as an Indian agent and fur trader. Local legends claim that on the night the Bleeckers' first child was born, Indians attacked the cabin in search of rum. Another tale has it that Bleecker made yearly trips to a secret cave filled with silver, emerging each time with a heavy satchel. Both stories seem highly improbable.

One thing is certain, that Bleecker was living in the area at a very early date. A letter from Kingston, dated 25 March 1788 and addressed to him at the 'Head of Bay Kinty,' reads: 'Dear Sir, Your sister was here and brought a pack of skins ... wishing you a pleasant passage and plenty of skins our dear Sir. (signed) Macaulay and Markland.' John's sister was the redoubtable Lucretia Bleecker Finkle of Bath.

When Catherine died, John eloped with her sister Mary. Yet another legend says that he paddled away with his bride, her father in hot pursuit. Captain Meyers was obviously unsuccessful. The couple settled down in Port Trent and when John died, at the age of forty-five, his widow took over the ferry. An order signed by Alexander Chisholm in 1808 allowed her the following charges:

For a man and horse, 8 pence
For a single person, 6 pence
For two or more persons, 4 pence each
Horned cattle, 4 pence per head
Sheep and swine, 2 pence per head
Every cart or carriage with 2 horses or oxen, 1 shilling, 3 pence

Sheldon Hawley came to Trenton in 1814 and prospered in the lumber business. He was active in civic and church affairs in the village, and encouraged the building of the first bridge across the Trent in 1833. This put an end to the ferry but enabled Weller's coaches to go through from York all the way to Kingston. In 1863, Hawley and his wife Nancy purchased the land at 72 Byron Street and immediately took out a mortgage. It is likely that they started the construction of the existing stone house shortly thereafter. Originally, the house was surrounded by apple orchards, and a curved driveway led up to the front door from gates near the road. The Hawley house has remained in excellent condition and only minor architectural changes have been made. The stone walls are twenty-one inches thick, and the windows have good panelling at their bases. A ghost who occasionally visited has not appeared for some time. It is reported that he once told a young visitor, 'Don't be afraid, little one. I won't hurt you.' The child's description of the ghost fitted perfectly that of a man who had died in the house some years before.

Although Rev. Dr John Strachan, Bishop of Toronto, is not usually remembered as a land speculator, he did own considerable property in Sidney Township, including the land on which the Hawley house later stood. Strachan planned to develop a settlement (called Ann Wood after his wife's maiden name) and had the area divided into lots. When the plan failed, he sold the land, which eventually became part of the town of Trenton. The names of Strachan and his wife are listed on the title to the Hawley house as owners until 1853.

The bishop and Hawley were partners in real estate transactions: the Strachan papers include letters to Hawley regarding conveyances and lot descriptions. The main subject of their correspondence, however, was a proposed church for Trenton. Thanks in large part to their efforts, St George's Church, at Byron and John Streets, was built in 1845–6. Hawley obviously admired the bishop, for he named one of his sons John Strachan Hawley. This son predeceased his parents and lies buried near them in the small cemetery by the stone church.

Sheldon Hawley house, 72 Byron Street

Bishop Strachan generously supported the building of St George's, but found it difficult. In a letter to Hawley he explained:

I remarked your proceedings about the church and have to state that it would not be convenient for me to pay my subscription all at once so it must be by installments of £25 for no salary having been made to the Bishopric I am put to great expense in discharging its duties that I feel much difficulty in keeping matters square.
John, Toronto
18 June, 1844

The rectory for St George's is west of the river, on King Street, east of Queen. Built in 1854, it was the only brick structure in Trenton until the 1870s. Bishop Strachan again helped to raise the necessary money. The rectory has lost its original verandah, which was replaced by a small portico. The third floor porch is also a later addition.

St George's Church, Byron and John Streets

The Gilmour Lumber building (which now houses the Quinte Planning Board) stands on Dundas Street East. It was built for a firm that, for the last half of the nineteenth century, prospered from the forests that made Trenton boom. From its first sawmill in 1852 it grew into a giant in the industry, with mills that handled up to 110,000 feet of lumber in a day. More recently, the old stone office building has served a variety of purposes. It was, for a while, a button factory which is said to have used each week twenty tons of clam shells imported from Kentucky. The building has also served as a school, hospital, library, and municipal offices.

During the heyday of the timber industry, the lumbermen added excitement and brought welcome business to the town. In *Life in the Clearings*, Susanna Moodie described how the logs reached the mills along the lake after their journey downriver from the forests:

It is a pretty sight, a large raft of timber extending perhaps for a quarter of a mile, gliding down the bay in tow of a steamer, decorated with red flags and green pine boughs and managed by a set of bold active fellows whose jovial songs waken up the echoes of the lonely woods ... The centre of the raft is generally occupied by a shanty and cooking apparatus and at night it presents an imposing spectacle seen by the red light of their fires as it glides beneath the shadow of some lofty bank.

The brick house at 22 McGill Street is built on land formerly owned by Allan Gilmour, part of the family's extensive land holdings in Trenton. Gilmour held the land for speculation. It is likely that the main portion of the house was not built until after 1874, when the property was bought by John W. Thompson. There may, however, have been a small house on the lot that was later incorporated into the larger building, for various architectural details in the interior suggest an earlier date. Joseph Shuter and his wife owned the lot from 1848 until they sold to Gilmour five years later. They may well have built a small house. Today, the building presents a curious melange of architectural styles but the result is quite satisfactory. On the gable end to the east, the roof has been extended to provide shelter for the second-floor gallery which extends across the width of the house. This is a recent addition.

The stone building that once served as a market for the farmers near Trenton has since become the town's police station. Unfortunately, the new use to which the building has been put does nothing to enhance what was once a fine example of classical revival architecture. The original windows may still be seen on the second floor, however, having happily escaped any attempts at renovation.

Just west of Trenton on Highway 2, near the road leading down to Carrying Place, are the homesteads of two early pioneers, George Abbott and his son-in-law John Little. Abbott came to Upper Canada from Massachusetts with his brothers Levi and William before the War of 1812. Levi subsequently returned to the United States, William settled near Ottawa, and George bought lot 7, concession A, Murray Township, near Trenton. He and his wife, Sarah Hennessey, had five children. When George died in 1848 he left his land to his son, Levi Lewis Abbott. It was Levi who built the fine stone house a short time later.

John Little bought the lot to the west of George Abbott (lot 8, concession A) in 1838. Eleven years later he took out a £250 mortgage on the property and probably began construction of his brick

22 McGill Street, on the west side of the Trent

house at about that time. John, an Irishman, had sailed to Canada with his three brothers sometime before 1833. The voyage took so long that in order to pay for their food, the brothers became sailors instead of passengers. After settling first near Lake of the Mountain, just east of Picton, they moved to Trenton, where they worked as carpenters. The same year that he purchased his land, John married Anna Margaret, George Abbott's second child. They had eleven children. John and Anna had a dream common to many pioneer families: they wanted to see each of their children established on the land, the one symbol of security. This dream came true. As they married, each of the eleven children received one hundred acres, a gift for the future from their parents.

Home of John and Anna Little, lot 8, concession A, Murray

8

Brighton-Presqu'ile

Brighton's main street follows fairly closely the route of the old York-Kingston Road. After its completion in 1817, stage coaches rumbled along its rutted surface at weekly or semi-weekly intervals, and inns were built to meet the needs of the weary passengers. Travel by stage coach was not for the faint-hearted. In her poem, 'The Corduroy Road,' Carrie M. Hoople described a typical journey over the corduroy roads:

Half a log, half a log
Half a log onward,
Shaken and out of breath,
Rode we and wondered.
Ours not to reason why
Ours but to clutch and cry
While onward we thundered.

In Brighton two inns near the corner of Main and Ontario Street supplied travellers with different kinds of accommodation, food, and drink. The first was Hodge's Tavern, a two-storey frame building at 156 Main Street. It was completed shortly after the road went through. Ira Hodges was not its first owner, but he was there by 1835 – his name appears in a list of innkeepers granted licences in that year. He was still in Brighton a quarter-century later; the 1861 census lists him as sixty years old, a bailiff, living with his wife Sarah Spafford and four children, and owning three horses, a cow, twelve sheep, seven pigs, and seven carriages for hire. By that time the inn was called Turkington's Hotel; it was run by a forty-three-year-old Irishman of that name, who lived there with his wife Eleanor and five children. Today the inn has been changed completely inside, but the exterior appears much as it did when it first welcomed travellers along the Danforth.

Across the road, on the southeast corner of Main and Ontario Streets, stands the former Temperance Hotel, an inn that provided travellers with alternative accommodation. Many of the hostelries of the day were rowdy and boisterous, the result of low-cost whiskey, and some of the passengers on the coach lines doubtlessly preferred a less stimulating environment. The Brighton *Sentinel*, in April 1853, mentioned that the Temperance Hotel was owned by B.M. Bettes.

The white frame house at 2 Ontario Street, at the southwest corner of the intersection with Main Street, was built around 1840

H.C. Bettes house, Main and Ontario Streets

for H.C. Bettes. In all likelihood he was related to the owner of the Temperance Hotel, but the connection is unknown. The house was sold to Ira Hodges in 1847 – probably the year that he sold his own inn to Turkington. Judging by the seven carriages that he kept for hire, Hodges maintained a livery business in his new location. It is believed locally that he also practised law in the office in the south part of the ground floor.

Certainly the finest building in Brighton is Proctor House, a magnificent Italianate structure just north of town, west of Young Street. Until recently this building stood abandoned and in danger of demolition. Its last residents, two Proctor sisters, had moved out in 1960. But a group of concerned citizens, unwilling to see the heritage home deteriorate further, organized a campaign which saw Proctor House re-opened as an official historic site in 1976. It is being restored to the 1840–80 period, and will be open as a museum five months of the year.

The man for whom this splendid house was built was John E. Proctor, one of Brighton's leading citizens. He owned mills, land, ships for the export of lumber, the Proctor Hotel, and a store. He was also, not surprisingly, a money-lender. The Proctor store's variety of merchandise is indicated by an advertisement in the Brighton *Sentinel* of 26 May 1854: 'J.E. Proctor – dealer in dry goods, groceries, liquors, boots, shoes, iron, paints, oils, patent medicine, glass and earthware. Cash paid for any quantity of good wheat and all kinds of grains, also sawed timber, ties, shingles and shingle bolts.'

Proctor's house was first called Millbank after his mills to the north of it. It must have been built between April 1867, when Proctor was assessed $500 on forty acres of cleared land, and April 1869, when the assessment jumped to $3,000 for the same forty acres 'with buildings.' The survey of property for assessment in those years was signed by John E. Proctor, Reeve.

The house is elegant. The front door, protected by a small portico, leads into a spacious entrance hall. At the far end of the hall, a graceful staircase curves up to the ballroom and bedrooms on the second floor. From there, a narrow flight of stairs leads to a belvedere and a breathtaking view of the lake and the surrounding country. All the interior trim is pine. Much of it has been painted and then brushed to give the appearance of oak. This required a skilled craftsman. The pine was first given a coat of yellow ochre, then another of raw umbre. Then it was brushed and varnished to pro-

Millbank, now Proctor House

duce the appearance of hardwood. The device may be found in some other houses of the period.

At the southeast corner of Main and Division Streets is a red brick commercial building. It is known as the Wade Block, after a physician who for many years had his offices and home there. Despite its name, the block was built by two previous owners, John Martin and Samuel Elmore Marsh, in the 1860s. It has always served as both office building and residence. Originally, an open winding staircase led from the ground-floor offices to the living quarters above. The ceilings are eleven feet high and handsome, and combined with round-headed windows that are similarly scaled to produce a spacious and elegant interior. The small balcony off the living room originally had a wood spindle railing, but this has been replaced with one of wrought iron.

South of Main Street are several small houses of interest. The neat brick house at 22 Napoleon Street has counterparts throughout

Wade Block, Main and Division Streets

the province but is a good example of a popular vernacular style. Its panelled door has side and transom lights and is flanked by two windows, perfectly symmetrically placed, which show panelling at the base; beneath the peaked gable is a gothic window. The property on which the house stands was bought by Solomore Boright in 1855 from Isaac Proctor's substantial holdings. Sixteen years later it was sold by Eunice Boright to Patrick Byrons. The house is a typical artisan's dwelling of the 1850s.

44 Division Street is said to have been the first brick house in Brighton. It was likely built during the 1840s by John Burr. A descendant of an early occupant recalls that it was owned for many years by a Mr Winn, but it is impossible to know whether this was Robert Winn the shoemaker who, in 1853, advertised his wares as being 'Cheap for Cash,' or Joseph or Samuel Winn, both of whom were mentioned in a later edition of the *Sentinel* that year as having letters waiting for them at the post office. At one time the house had

22 Napoleon Street

a partially enclosed verandah, but otherwise it remains much as it was originally.

William Butler was born in Compton, New Hampshire, in 1800. Twenty years later he settled in Cramahe Township, moving to Brighton sometime before 1848. In Brighton he built a grist mill and a carding and fulling mill. (Fulling was a process by which wool cloth was shrunk and thickened by means of steam heat). In 1848 he built a spacious brick house at 211 Prince Edward Street. Butler owned a great deal of other land in the area as well, and in October 1853 he subdivided and sold much of it. The *Sentinel* reported: 'Mr Butler's sale of village lots realized over £1,000. Between 90 and 100 lots were sold. In the afternoon about 60 persons sat down to a sumptuous dinner in Mr Butler's splendid mansion. A better dinner, perhaps, was never prepared in Brighton.'

The Butler 'mansion' is indeed a good-sized house. When it was first completed, Butler, his wife Elizabeth, and two children lived in

William Butler house, 211 Prince Edward Street

it along with several servants. By the time of the 1861 census, there were four children. In that year, Butler had $16,000 invested in his lumber business, which annually produced 200,000 feet of lumber.

Much of the interior trim in the Butler house is of white pine that has been painted to resemble walnut. A craftsman was brought from Boston to perform the work.

When the present owner purchased Butler Farm, the house was suffering from years of neglect. Thoughtless tenants had left doors and windows open to the weather. Floors and walls were severely damaged, and the original hand-carved balustrade had been torn apart for firewood. Restoration is now happily almost complete.

In 1849, while the Butlers were building their handsome house, the Methodist Church at Prince Edward and Chapel Streets was also rising – on land donated by William Butler. The simple brick edifice, with its white steeple rising above the town, is very much a part of its surroundings. Its appearance is in keeping with the other

Trinity-St Andrew's United Church

early buildings, simple and unpretentious. The church is now known as Trinity-St Andrew's United Church.

William and Elizabeth's son, Charles Butler, married Marie Smith, who came from Smithfield, a village just east of Brighton. Marie's ancestor, Joseph Smith, had left England and settled in New York State during the first half of the eighteenth century. His sons, Jesse and John, fought on opposing sides during the Revolutionary War, Jesse with the British and John with the Americans. Jesse and his father eventually returned to England, but John stayed and married Mary McDowall. Her brother, Rev. Robert McDowall, was a minister serving parishioners between York and Brockville before 1800. He urged Mary and John to settle in Canada. This they did, becoming the first settlers in the village that later was named after them.

Robert McDowall Smith, one of their seven children, built the two-storey frame house on the north side of Smithfield's Main Street – part of the original Danforth Road. The house has changed substantially over the years: the small-paned windows have been replaced, and the three stone fireplaces that once warmed the house have gone. At one time, a small room at the rear was used by an itinerant shoemaker when he visited the village. The wide verandah on the front of the house was added early in the 1900s.

To the south of Brighton, Presqu'ile Point juts into Lake Ontario. Presqu'isle, the French for peninsula (literally, 'almost an island'), is now a provincial park. Many years ago, however, it was thought that it would become one of the most influential communities on the lake. One tragic accident put an end to that future.

In 1802, the government of the day decided to make what is now Presqu'ile the capital of the District of Newcastle, with a town called Newcastle at Presqu'ile Point. Its accessibility by water made it an ideal location. Plans were drawn up, and a courthouse and jail built – the first government buildings in the proposed town. Then in 1804 the schooner *Speedy*, en route from York, was lost during a heavy storm. On board were government and court officials and an Indian who was being brought to stand trial at Presqu'ile for murder. All perished; no sign of the vessel was ever found. Soon after the tragedy, Newcastle was abandoned as a seat of government. Instead, Cobourg became the capital of the district. Its harbour was felt to be less hazardous.

While several families were living on Presqu'ile Point when the

Speedy was lost, only two early buildings remain. Both are log buildings, and both could date from the early 1800s.

On lot 10, Broken Front, Brighton Township, almost hidden from the road by fir trees, is the larger of the two. It is said to have been one of the first buildings between Kingston and York – a statement almost impossible to prove or disprove. Whatever its exact date, the house must be indeed very early and still is in excellent condition. The dormers which face the lake and the chimney appear to be later additions.

The second of the houses is to the east, on lot 8, Broken Front, Brighton. Until a few years ago it was covered with siding, but the log construction has since been revealed. Little is known of the history of these houses, though they could have belonged to any of the four families living on the point at the beginning of the century – the Simpsons, Rogers, Gibsons, and Selkirks.

At the end of Presqu'ile Point stands a lighthouse, built in 1840 to

Robert McDowall Smith house, Smithville

warn the many schooners on the lake away from the rocks. Stories abound of shipwrecks in the area. Many of the ships are said to have been carrying gold or other treasure when they sank. The stories, of course, lose nothing in the telling.

Near the entrance to Presqu'ile Point, a cairn commemorates the area's first settler, Obediah Simpson. He was a Loyalist from Wilmington, North Carolina, and came to Upper Canada by way of Nova Scotia. In 1796 he arrived at Presqu'ile harbour, bringing with him his twelve-year-old son John and a team of oxen. After building a small log house and a shelter for the cattle, he donned his snowshoes and walked back to Adolphustown, where he had left the rest of his family. Young John remained alone to care for the oxen. He was there from February until his family arrived in April to begin clearing the land.

Just west of Brighton, on the south side of Highway 2, is an imposing structure known locally and to travellers as the White House.

Log house, lot 10, Presqu'ile Point

Although it was not built until the 1870s, this remarkable building played such an important part in the life of Brighton that its story must be included here.

John Eyre, a local lawyer who came from England and began to practise in Brighton in 1853, was its first owner. He supplied the plans for it, and lived in it until his death. The house had many refinements unusual for its day, including a privy with water which was pumped from a nearby windmill. In 1898 it was purchased by Samuel G.M. Nesbitt, a flamboyant local businessman who had made his money in the fruit-canning industry. He added the portico and the tower to the front and, in the 1920s, made elaborate interior renovations. Over the existing hardwood floors he installed new parquet flooring of cherry, maple, walnut, and oak. He imported from Europe mahogany doors and new mantelpieces – one of peach-coloured marble to complement the parlour's gold-and-white decor. From the large ballroom on the third floor, he installed a circular

Presqu'ile Point lighthouse

wrought iron staircase leading to the top of the tower. Nesbitt and his friends occasionally played cards in the small tower room.

In 1937, the White House became Rene's White House Hotel. It was operated by Irene Dixon, who had worked as a housekeeper for Nesbitt's son, Edmund. As proprietress she dressed always in starched white, and insisted that the waiters dress in white as well. Guests at the hotel over the years included Irene Castle, Bing Crosby, Walt Disney, and Barbara Ann Scott.

The barn at the rear of the White House was built by Nesbitt in 1917. Its walls are panelled with tongue-and-groove siding and, in Nesbitt's day, lace curtains hung at the windows. It must have been one of the 'prettiest' barns in Ontario.

Along the highway between Brighton and Colborne are three early buildings worthy of note. The first, on lot 6, concession 2, Brighton Township was an old two-storey frame inn owned by John Proctor's father, Isaac. Like Hodge's hotel in town, it was built

The White House, a Brighton landmark

shortly after the York-Kingston Road was completed. John's grandfather, Josiah, may even have operated the inn at one time, for in 1819 he had an innkeeper's licence and was fined £10 for an infraction of the regulations governing taverns. Josiah was a local figure of note, remembered both for great strength and great size – in his later years he is said to have weighed nearly five hundred pounds.

Further west the Danforth Road passes through the small community of Salem. Today the area is chiefly agricultural. In the middle of the last century, however, it supported five mills; and like other communities of its size Salem thrived as its mills thrived. The Salem United Church (lot 21, concession 1, Cramahe Township) was built in 1861 of lumber planed in a local mill. The basically simple design has been embellished by the addition of a tower and a gothic window over the door.

The substantial white frame house on lot 22, concession 2, Cramahe, was the home of a Salem miller. In 1809 the land was held by

Miller's house in Salem, lot 22, concession 2, Cramahe

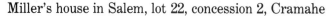

John Frint. In 1816 it passed to Henry Frint. By 1846 the family spelling had changed to Freint and by 1853, when an advertisement appeared in the Brighton *Sentinel*, the spelling had changed once more, a confusing but common occurrence.

FOR SALE

That splendid WATER POWER on the main road, two miles east of the village of Colborne, so well known as the Frent's Mills, Property the best privilege for Flouring Mills or a Factory in the County having 23 feet head and fall – with a never failing stream of water. There is ... an excellent Sawmill in active production, with Flume nearly new and sufficiently large to admit water for extensive machinery. There are 31 acres of land with good Blacksmith Shop, two Dwelling Houses and several out Houses etc. connected with the premises.

The house was built in 1850. Its size and design suggest the prosperity that could attend settlement on a prime site with a good stream.

9

Colborne

Major-General Sir John Colborne was lieutenant-governor of Upper Canada from 1828 to 1836. In his honour, the village of Keeler's Tavern changed its name. (One family in the province, according to Dr Canniff, went further; it named triplet boys born during the governor's tenure Sir, John, and Colborne.) The change in the name of the community did not however affect the dominance of three successive generations of Joseph Keelers – 'Old Joe,' 'Young Joe,' and 'Little Joe' – in Colborne's settlement, growth, and industry from the 1790s until 1885. Today the home of Joseph Keeler II on Church Street attests to their economic success in the era of Colborne's greatest prosperity.

'Old Joe,' a Loyalist from Vermont, settled in the 1790s at Lakeport (known initially as Cramahe Harbour, Colborne Harbour, or Cat Hollow). Shortly afterward, he was followed by a group of settlers. They included Aaron Greeley, an American surveyor who came at Keeler's request to lay out a town site. But it is 'Young Joe' who is considered Colborne's founder. He was its first merchant, opening a store in 1815, and its first postmaster. He donated land for a public square, and to both the Methodist (now United) and Presbyterian churches. He was also justice of the peace.

Keeler's Church Street house is almost identical to the Barnum house in Grafton. The Keeler house was built about 1820, about the same time as the Barnum house; it is possible they were built with the same inspiration. Eliakim Barnum's home is nationally known, however, while the Keeler house has been given much less attention.

It has long been considered a later copy – one of many in the Grafton-Colborne-Cobourg area – but it is the only one with the same intricate detail of neo-classic trim as on the Barnum house. The original first floor contained a hall and adjacent living room in the central portion, a sitting room and library in the two wings, and the dining room and kitchen at the rear. The upper storey contained three bedrooms off the hall. Superb craftsmanship is evident in the carving over the door, on the pilasters, cornices, mouldings, mantel, and stairs, and in every small detail of interior trim.

The Keelers bought the property on which the house stands in 1812; it was part of a Crown grant made to George Palmer nine years earlier. In 1824, the family subdivided the two hundred acres, presumably to encourage the development of the neighbourhood. 'Old Joe' died in 1834 in his son's house, aged seventy-seven. By the 1850s, 'Young Joe' had decided to build another house, on the hill overlooking Colborne. Kelwood, many years in construction, was

Home of Joseph Keeler, Church Street

planned in the grand manner, with parquet floors, marble mantels, large dining and drawing rooms, servants' quarters, and an elaborate series of walkways. Keeler presented the Church Street house to his daughter, but raised his son, in Kelwood. 'Little Joe' became the Member of Parliament for East Northumberland, established a newspaper, and acted as its editor. Kelwood was destroyed by fire in 1911.

The Keeler name is associated with another building that survives on the northeast corner of King and Parliament (lot 28, concession 2, Cramahe) in East Colborne. It was once Keeler's Tavern, for which the community was first named. According to the District of Newcastle records, 'Old Joe' was fined £2 in 1808 for operating a still; apparently he had a business well before the opening of the York Road in 1816. But the white frame house which is presumed to be the inn stands on land which did not come into the Keeler family until 1832. Was it built by one of the previous owners? (Schuyler

Former Keeler Tavern, King and Parliament Streets

Hodges or Jacob Loomis would be the most likely candidates.) Did Keeler have an inn on some other site? Or did he operate more informally?

At one time the house was covered with insulbrick. Restoration in the 1970s revealed not only the original frame siding but four unexpected windows which had been covered, no doubt to preserve heat within. The house now displays all nine windows, five above and four below in a typical Loyalist style.

Across the road is a house which dates from the period of the War of 1812. It served as a barracks and later a school. In 1828 it was turned over to King's College as part of the land grant intended as a financial base for that institution, which became the University of Toronto. In 1851, the university sold the property to Peleg Wood. The memoirs of Elizabeth Goslee Grover, who was present, recall the day when Peleg brought his bride, 'a pretty girl with dark eyes,' to his home. Twenty young girls and men from Belleville accompanied them. The party danced to 'violin reels and country dances – all the girls wore white caps and the men in dancing would spring from the floor, slap their heels two or three times and fall into place – kicking dancing steps, that was the style then and Mrs Wood was called the best dancer in the settlement.'

The house was built with a verandah on the sides and French windows, all of which have been removed. It has all the features of the solid construction of the early 1800s. The exterior mouldings are simple and heavy. The door in the second-storey verandah is a feature typical of inn construction. While it was owned by King's College it was leased for income, but it is impossible to be sure which lessees occupied the land in that period. In view of the style of construction and location – right on the Danforth Road – could it have been used as an inn? To take speculation one step further, could it have been Keeler's first inn?

An octagonal house, north on Parliament Street past Keeler's Inn, was built by Reuben Scott, an iron founder. The unusual shape was promoted by Orson Fowler, who believed that both health and disposition were greatly improved in an eight-sided house. A book by Fowler was found in the house, indicating that Scott was familiar with the theories, discussed in chapter 14.

At 3 King Street West is a white frame house which was the home of John Steele and his wife, Mary Spalding. Steele came to Canada from Greenock, Scotland, in 1820, lived for a while in Montreal, and then moved to Colborne, where he was involved in business ventures with Joseph Keeler. He published a Colborne newspaper, the *Northumberland Pilot,* and was later involved with the Port Hope *Watchman.* A staunch Presbyterian, he protested against the then-established position of the Anglican church, helped found Queen's University, and was a member of its first Board.

Between 1831 and 1835 Steele bought parts of the land at the town centre which had been granted by the Crown to John Ogden in 1809. The present frame house could have been on the site already, for its simplicity and interior detailing relate to an earlier period. Mary Steele may have been writing from the house when she addressed her friend Susan Greeley in Haldimand, on 7 February 1831:

My haste must apologize for my abruptness while I say that I would like to get that girl Miss Smith and that I would wish her to begin next week with me if possible perhaps better to say come on Saturday as I would never encourage going or coming on the Sabbath. I forgot to mention I should expect to pay her out of the store and of course to let her get shoes and the like where we are dealing. Please give my best regards to your dear mother.

In 1843 John and Mary Steele sold their Colborne property and moved to Grafton to live in a red brick house beside Mary's father, Thomas Spalding. Later they moved to Port Hope. A surviving letter to John Steele there in 1851 expressed sympathy on Mary's death.

The red brick house adjacent to the Steele house was at one time part of the Steele holdings, but by 1861 belonged to Cuthbert Cumming. It remained in his family until 1910. Cumming was a Scottish-born fur trader with the North West Company and the Hudson's Bay Company. He became a chief trader in 1827, was married in the northland in the early 1840s to Jane McMurray, served at Fort Pelly in the Swan River district, and in 1844 retired and moved to Colborne. At the time of the census of 1861, he was seventy years old. Jane was forty-seven years old, and they had three children, the oldest fourteen, the youngest five. The single-storey Cumming house was probably built of locally-made bricks, as there were at least three brickyards operating in Colborne by the mid-1800s.

Colborne's United (formerly Wesleyan Methodist) church was

built in the 1860s to replace an 1830 structure. The bricks came from the Keeler brickyard.

The Presbyterians built their handsome church, St Andrew's, in 1830 as well, hauling the stone from a Lakeport quarry over rugged roads. John Steele was one of the first Presbyterian trustees. The ministry in those days was a hazardous occupation: the Presbyterian minister in the area drowned crossing the ice of the Bay of Quinte in 1834 while travelling between his parishes. A letter to Steele from Rev. Robert McDowall described the tragedy: the minister, a Mr Miller, had been 'very desirous to meet his engagements in your region ... I gave him written directions. He did speak about going up on the ice all the way to Belleville as it was much easier travelling on ice than on land. I told him of the danger and that I would not venture to do it though I was much more acquainted with the dangerous places.'

The land and lumber used in the construction of Trinity Anglican

3 King Street West, home of John and Mary Spalding Steele

Church were given by J.D. Goslee in 1843 and the church opened in
1846; Bishop Strachan attended the ceremony. Goslee's daughter,
Elizabeth Goslee Grover, told the story of her family in memoirs
that were written in 1896, her eighty-first year.

Elizabeth's grandmother, born Ann Schuyler, was a niece of
Philip Schuyler, one of George Washington's most respected gener-
als; Ann's father was himself a member of Washington's army and
Washington was her godfather and a frequent visitor in the Schuyler house. Matthew Goslee, Elizabeth's grandfather, was the son of
a wealthy American family who supported the King's cause and
forfeited all his property in the new United States. They often told
her, when she was a child, of their first meeting. On 27 August 1776,
Ann was alone in the family home near Albany listening to the dis-
tant sounds of battle. Her mother was dead; and by the end of the
day she learned her father and brother had both been killed as well.
There was a chance the British troops would burn the house. With

Presbyterian Church

her father's servant as companion, she rode off to seek her uncle. But the army tents they finally found were the enemy's. 'I was in the Jersey woods,' Ann would tell the young Elizabeth, 'and before me stood a tall handsome soldier in a red coat, one sleeve gone but the arm wrapped in a bloody bandage.' The tall handsome redcoat was of course Matthew Goslee. He escorted Ann to a spot near her uncle's camp, and Ann stayed with General Schuyler in Albany until the end of the war. One night the general returned home escorting Matthew Goslee as his personal prisoner. In time Ann and Matthew were married and left with the Loyalists. In the Colborne area they built a large log house. They always kept the saddle which Ann had used on the day they met.

J.D. Goslee was their son. He became a timber merchant in Colborne. His son, George, was an insurance agent in the 1850s. They were listed together on the title of the red brick house which stands, with a most impressive vista, on the north side of King Street, back

Trinity Anglican Church

from the Kingston Road. The building has elaborate bargeboard on its peaked gable and eaves. In due course it was bought by George Webb, a cabinetmaker and general merchant. The present owners, whose family have occupied the house for three generations, believe that the barn and shed behind the house were used as a cooperage for an apple-packing business.

Also associated with the Goslee family is the Registry Office in the village centre. It was built in the 1850s on land given by John M. Grover, who married Elizabeth Goslee. Grover became the registrar for East Northumberland. He and Elizabeth built Seaton Hall, a substantial brick building set back from the road just west of the Webb house. It was named after Sir John Colborne, Lord Seaton.

The many white frame houses in Lakeport recall the years when that community was an active harbour. In the schooner days, lake captains lived in what was then called Colborne Harbour or Cat Hollow. Schooners were built at the shipyard, and shipments of

Webb house, King Street

grain left from two large wharves – Keeler's and Campbell's. A plaster mill, grist mill, sawmill, flour mill, and distillery provided other cargo for the vessels. The ruins of Keeler's mill can still be seen on the Colborne-Lakeport road. Like the Presbyterian church, it was built of stone from the nearby Lakeport quarry.

One property in Lakeport is associated with both the Keeler and Campbell names. Joseph Keeler received the Crown grant for it in 1809, and according to the assessment records lived up to the 1830s in a frame house of one storey on lots 1 and 2, concessions A and B, Haldimand. His home probably formed the central portion of the large white frame house by the lake, owned by the Campbell family in the 1840s. Campbell enlarged the building, adding a second storey.

West of Lakeport, on lot 11, concession B, Haldimand, stands Lakeview. George Shields, who had previously lived in Grafton, owned the property by 1846 and had thirty-five of its fifty acres

Registry office: the land was given by the first registrar, John Grover

under cultivation. Between 1859 and 1863 his assessment jumped from $450 to $1700, so it is probable that the house was built between those years. It is shown in the 1878 county atlas as a fine frame building on a thriving farm. In a letter from Lakeview dated 1881, Shields outlined his plans for his farm: 'I was over at the States a couple of weeks ago and I engaged in the tree and flower business. I will be at it I think next week or next month. I don't know how it will go selling but I am going to try it anyway. I thrashed last week and had 16 bushels of wheat, over 200 of barley and 170 of oats. I suppose you have heard of me letting the place on shares.'

Ruins of Keeler mill, on the Colborne-Lakeport road

Lakeview, home of George Shields

10

Grafton

In 1798, when Haldimand was only slightly advanced from the wilderness, the Baptists of that township were organized in sufficient numbers to hold regular services and plan construction of a church by the lake. Their first building near Lakeport served the congregation until 1824, when the present simple frame Wicklow Church was built on lot 13, concession A, Haldimand. The baptistry behind the lectern is the original one into which candidates for baptism would step; it extends into the back room. The carefully preserved church records reveal some of the lesser-known aspects of pioneer life – including the way arguments might be settled.

16 January 1803: Brothers and sisters met according to appointment a committy chosen to settle a Difficulty Between Br. Hinmon and Br. Palmer Crandall and chose 6 members which found them both Very hard towards Each other which Committy concluded to set them both aside till they reformed agreed on by the Ch.

26 February 1803: Church meeting held in Cramahe after Renewing Covenant Brother Hinmon Comforward and took up his Ground and was Received by the Church.

In March 1844 John Montgomery Campbell advertised for tenders for the construction of a granary and repairs to a distillery on lot 20, concession 1, Haldimand, just east of Grafton – a property he had bought about a year and a half earlier, and turned into an enterprise which provided a large portion of the five hundred casks of whiskey exported from Grafton Harbour in 1847. Campbell was initially associated in business with his neighbours to the north, the Standly family, and later with W.F. Pym. The Campbell and Pym distillery absorbed up to two thousand bushels of grain per day and provided work for so many men that cottages were built and the area became known as Campbelltown.

The port of Grafton was thriving as a trading centre. Lake ships called to pick up shipments of flour, lumber, plaster, whiskey, and other products. Around the harbour, homes rose along with a mill and cooper and blacksmith shops. Many mills also operated in nearby Shelter Valley. Grafton village boasted distilleries, flour mills, a brickyard, stores, and associated trades as well as churches and a healthy agricultural base.

The house Campbell built on lot 19, concession 1 is called Stillbrook. It has high ceilings, pine floors, detailed woodwork, and

Wicklow Baptist Church, lot 13, concession A, Haldimand

numerous fireplaces. One fireplace on the second floor was constructed with a window over the mantel – the flue runs up the right side. The most striking feature of the house is the spacious hall, with an imposing staircase at the far end which leads to a pair of French doors on the landing. These doors open onto a mystery. On their other side is a narrow passage-way which leads to a ballroom with a cathedral ceiling – the upper storey of an early inn. This inn and the main house are attached by the passage, but the purpose is a puzzle. Did the inn always rest on this site and did Major Campbell incorporate it into his home when it was built in the late 1840s? Was the inn moved by Campbell from some other location on the Danforth or was there an early road here? One possible explanation for the passageway is that it was built so that ladies could reach the ballroom without having to walk through the first-floor tavern.

South of Stillbrook is a brick house now painted white, on lot 20,

Stillbrook, lot 19, concession 1, Haldimand; staircase and doors to passageway in Stillbrook

concession 1. Campbell bought the property from David J. Smith and Maxwell Strange in 1844. The house must have been the residence of an important member of the business partnership – perhaps Pym or the manager. Both Campbell and Pym are listed for purposes of assessment. But by 1863 their names had disappeared: their fortunes declined and they returned to England, their birthplace.

The *Northumberland and Durham Atlas* of 1878 refers to Blink Bonnie, east of Grafton on lot 21, concession 1, as the home of William Mellis. It was built by John Taylor, who kept a general store in Grafton, was postmaster, and supplied Campbell and Pym with lumber from a mill he owned in Eddystone. He supported the Grafton and Haldimand Moral Society and the Agricultural Society. The property, part of a Crown grant to King's College, was purchased in 1847 by John Campbell, who sold it to Taylor in 1856. The brick and stucco house was built in the following year. The portico, verandah, and dormer at the front are of a later date, as is the rear extension. Over the years the house has been called Heathfield, Twin Gables, and more recently Canada House.

As the Danforth Road entered Grafton from the east, it turned south to the lake at Benlock Road. In choosing this route, Asa Danforth was probably following an early Indian trail which led to a fishing ground. This trail linked up with a road along the lake which pre-dated the Danforth. From the lake, the Danforth headed north past St Andrew's United Church to the open doors of the inns, taverns, and general store in the village centre. The Danforth route carried military traffic during the War of 1812. In the Grafton area, the log house owned by David McGregor Rogers served as a depot for the distribution of provisions.

The Rogers family had been connected with the military for most of its history. Perhaps the most famous member was David's uncle, Robert Rogers, an American who founded Rogers' Rangers during the Seven Years' War and helped defeat the French in North America. In 1779 he raised a new corps, the King's Rangers, for the Revolutionary War. He was its lieutenant-colonel and David's father, James Rogers, commanded its 2nd Battalion. At war's end James took his own family and his men and their families to Fredericksburgh and later to Hallowell, Prince Edward County. David moved to Grafton and in 1808 was living in a house of rough logs; he had cultivated only sixteen of his 1,400 acres. By 1813 he had built a two-storey frame house. This house no longer stands but a family house built by a grandson is located well back from the Danforth on the original Rogers property (lot 25, concession 1, Haldimand). David served for many years as a member of the Legislative Assembly. He died in 1824.

Three documents from the area give an idea of Rogers' role and of the pressures during the War of 1812. On 27 February 1812, Isaac Brock appointed Rogers to arrest 'such Person or Persons as may appear ... by words or actions or other behaviour ... hath given just cause to suspect that he, she or they ... is about to alienate the minds of His Majesty's subjects ... with seditious intent to disturb the tranquility.' In April 1813 Sir Roger Sheaffe, commander-in-chief of British forces after Brock's death at Queenston Heights, wrote from Rogers' home to Sir George Prevost, 'Firing from Niagara was heard in the afternoon of the 28th and both yesterday and today the firing at York though the wind was fresh from the east was heard even at this distance.' On 27 August 1814 Major Rogers wrote to a Lieut.-Col. Peters at Hodges Inn, Cramahe, 'A detachment of York Militia are on their way from York with 79 prisoners. I am ordered to get ready a guard of at least 30 men to relieve them and request you will furnish me with the men as soon as possible to be at the Court House tomorrow evening.' The letter from Sir Roger Sheaffe now is in the Public Archives of Canada; the other two documents are among the Rogers Papers in the Ontario Archives.

The white frame St Andrew's Presbyterian Church on the Danforth Road was built in 1844. Some years ago the floor was raised to create a basement and some windows were changed, but beyond this it is unaltered. The Presbyterian settlers of the area were served first by a travelling missionary and then by a minister appointed for Colborne and Grafton.

Two white frame houses stand on the east side of the Danforth Road as it curves north from the lake past St Andrew's into the village centre. Both are connected with descendants of James Lawless, one of Grafton's early shopkeepers. They were built in the 1820s and came into the possession of the Lawless family at a later date. James Lawless came to Canada from Ireland in 1821 and settled in Montreal, where he became a school teacher. In 1835 he moved to Grafton and operated the general store which faces the Mansion House Hotel.

Six inns were operating between 1815 and 1845 in Grafton, providing lodging, drink, and a meeting place for local residents and travellers. The only two remaining are the present Grafton Hotel in the village centre and Spalding's Inn at the west end of the village.

The Grafton Hotel was first called Pepper's Tavern. Reports of meetings held there show that the pioneer's hands were not always on the plough. A letter to the Cobourg *Star* in 1832 described a gathering which undertook to decide an official name for the village. 'After the business of the day was closed we were regaled in Mr Pepper's best style and among numerous toasts given on the occasion were the following:– The village of Grafton, the King and Constitution, Sir John Colborne and the Province of Upper Canada, May nae war be among us, the Constitution under which we live, and many others equally loyal and patriotic,' all of which produced 'cordiality and good feeling.' The name chosen honoured the former home of John Grover, Grafton, Massachusetts. Grover's name and that of his wife appear on the 1804 census.

St Andrew's Church, on the Danforth Road

In 1832 a meeting was called at Pepper's Tavern to form a society to combat 'those acts of intemperance that so much degrade human nature and sink it below the beasts of the field – deception in word and deed, contention and brawling, speaking disrespectfully of the Deity, the Christian religion, the King or those in authority, drunkeness' and finally 'amusement, worldly conversation or labour on the Sabbath.' The high aims of the society were embodied in its official title; the 'Grafton and Haldimand Moral Society for the Suppression of vice etc.' According to a local paper the society uttered its last 'tut-tut' in the same year it was founded. Pepper's also held a very successful dinner for the St Andrew's Society in 1834. The toasts given surpassed those which marked the naming of Grafton two years earlier: 'The day and all who honour it, the King, the Queen and Royal Family, His Majesty's Ministers, the Land O'Lakes, the Land we live in, Sir John Colborne, Wallace and Bruce, names dear to Scotland and to liberty, the Parish Schools of Scotland, the mem-

Pepper's Tavern, now the Grafton Hotel

ory of Sir Walter Scott, the bonnie lassies of two worlds, May care and trouble never fash, but mirth and joy be wi' us a', The Rose, Shamrock and Thistle, Old England, The Emerald Isle, Speedy union to every lad and lass.' When a letter was read from H. Ruttan apologising for his absence, his health was drunk as well.

The Grafton Town Hall, on lot 23, concession 1 replaced the Mansion House as the centre for some business meetings and formal balls after its opening in 1859. On that occasion the Grafton Brass Band gave a concert in the Hall, with the assistance of the Grafton Serenaders and other amateur performers. Although alterations on the lower level detract from what was once a handsome structure, the building is historic.

Until 1892 the Anglican rectory, on lot 22, concession A, Haldimand, was instantly recognizable as a replica of the Barnum house west of Grafton. In that year it was turned on its site and the wings removed. Now the side which originally faced west faces the road

St George's Church rectory

and the parish church, St George's. The verandah was added when the wing was removed. Church records state that the house was built in the early 1840s by J.C. Hogaboom and became the rectory for the Grafton-Colborne Mission in 1849. Grafton was the home of a number of prosperous families who settled their rector in what was then a handsome colonial house.

The church cemetery has recently been restored. Now the stones marking the graves of the Rogerses and the Barnums can be seen, along with that of a Hudson's Bay factor, Mackenzie, who retired to the Grafton area. Much of the history of Grafton can be read on the stones in the cemeteries of St George's and St Andrew's churches.

When the Danforth Road opened in 1816, Spalding's Inn was advertised as the halfway house between York and Kingston. Within a couple of years, court records show, Thomas Spalding had to pay £10 in inkeepers' fines – such fines being a common source of government revenue until innkeeping licenses began to be systematically issued. The inn (on lot 25, concession A, Haldimand) and its neighbour to the east are two of the finest nineteenth-century brick buildings in the province.

It is possible that the rear portion of the present red brick building was the first inn but census records and assessment rolls for Haldimand Township suggest that the main structure was built much later. According to the original assessment rolls, Spalding was already living in Haldimand in 1803 with his wife and two young children, but the 1810–11 rolls still have him living in a 'house of round logs.' From 1815 to 1834 they show his residence as 'frame under two storey with additional fireplace' (one fireplace was considered the norm); but in 1835 he owns a 'two-storey brick building with additional fireplaces' – the house presumably was built in the intervening year. The texture and mellow colour of the bricks (perhaps from the Spalding brickyards located on the property) demand notice. On the side they have been laid in a style called Flemish Bond, with headers and stretchers alternating. The interior woodwork speaks of hours of skilled hand carving. The house even has a story of buried treasure. Like many such legends connected with early days on the Danforth, it is concerned with a payload robbery. A coachman whose destination was Spalding's Inn was warned of robbers lying in wait for him. He turned away, was pursued, and eluded the robbers long enough to bury the gold. Whether the story is true, the reader may judge.

To the east of Spalding's Inn is the Steele house, the home of Thomas Spalding's daughter Mary and her husband, John Steele of Colborne. Spalding was anxious to have his daughter – one of eight children – near him and is said to have urged the young couple to move there. They quickly became involved in local life. A girl's boarding school, run by Mrs Steele, is said to have been held in the house in the 1840s, and the Steeles opened their home for community events such as meetings of the Grafton Female Association, which undoubtedly did not wish to use the local tavern as was the custom. The house and a half-acre were later sold for £600 to John Dougald Cameron, a Hudson's Bay factor who retired there with his wife, a Cree Indian he met and married at the Red River.

South of Spalding's Inn (on lot 25, Broken Front A), is The Maples, built in 1864 by William Webster of Cold Kirby, Yorkshire, for his second wife. William had come to Canada in 1822 when he was a year old, with his parents and sister. In 1846 he married Sarah

Spalding's Inn, lot 25, concession A, Haldimand

Ann Hare. Like many another woman of the time, she died shortly after the birth of a child – their third. Nine years later William, then forty-three, married Annie Clark of Grafton, built The Maples, and produced twelve more children, the last when he was sixty-two. The Webster house was built of bricks made locally. The small porch is a later addition.

As Asa Danforth's road curves northwest out of Grafton it passes a reminder of plank roads and stage coaches – the toll-gate house for the Grafton-Cobourg road. The Cobourg and Grafton Road Company was incorporated in 1847, and was enpowered to collect tolls to help pay the cost of a road paved with planks – a surface far preferable to ruts and potholes. Tolls continued until 1919, when the government took over the road. The last keepers of the gate used the foundation and part of the original structure to form the present building, on the north side of the road past Spalding's Inn. The rear, frame portion is the old toll house from which the porch was re-

The Maples, south of Spalding's Inn

moved. Older residents recall the rates: 'Pigs and sheep ½ cent, cows 1 cent, 4 cents for horse and buggy.' The tolls were collected in a cup held out on the end of a long stick.

West of Grafton village, on lot 26, concession 1, Haldimand, stands a house which has been called one of the finest examples of colonial architecture in Canada. The property was bought in 1812 by Eliakim Barnum, a native of Vermont born in 1783. In the following year, according to the assessment rolls, sixty of the three hundred acres were cultivated, and Barnum was living in a one-story frame house. In 1821 he added more property and a two-storey frame building – the present one. Local legend states that the first Barnum house was accidentally burned one Christmas by troops billeted there. If such an accident did happen, it must have been to an early log building which Barnum replaced with the single-storey structure.

Despite his American birth, Barnum was not a republican. Rather, he was an active member, and chairman in 1836, of the Haldimand Constitution Society, a group which opposed the reform politics of William Lyon Mackenzie. He was also active on the local Harbour Board. As the father of one child, he petitioned in 1820 for the first school and for a teacher to be paid fifteen dollars a month and 'sufficient and decent board, washing and lodging.' His own wealth came from a flour mill and a distillery. The mill was close to that of Stephen Hare on lot 27, concession 1, probably the first in the area.

Barnum called his neo-classic house The Poplars. The box-shaped central portion is flanked by single-storey wings. The sides are clapboard, but the front has a flat finish more conducive to the ornamentation. The placing of the door is in sharp contrast to the symmetry of Georgian houses like the Fairfield White House in Ernestown, on the Bath Road.

Throughout the area there are many replicas of the Barnum house. One is located northwest of Grafton, up the Gully Road on the old Danforth. The Anglican rectory in Grafton has already been mentioned, as has the Keeler house in Colborne. Since both Barnum and the Keelers came from Rutland, Vermont, their houses may have reflected the same local architecture and been built with knowledge of the same plans.

Eliakim Barnum's house, The Poplars, lot 26, concession 1, Haldimand

The area north of Grafton, in particular the part known as Academy Hill, north of Highway 401, was the first home of the Massey family. Tombstones at the top of the hill overlooking Lake Ontario remember ancestors of Hart Massey, founder of the Massey-Ferguson empire, Vincent Massey, Canada's first native-born governor-general, and Raymond Massey, the actor. A nearby Massey home of the 1860s has had additions made in a whimsical fashion to the point where it resembles a castle. An earlier Massey home built of stone stands near the burial ground.

On the Grafton-Cobourg section of the Danforth, to the north and west of Grafton (lot 4, concession 1, Hamilton), is the Halfway House, one of the earliest buildings on the old York road. It was built shortly after 1800. It served as a popular resting place for travellers. Today insulbrick completely conceals the log construction. Only the simple lines, the splendid door to the second-floor veran-

The Mallorys' Regency cottage, lot 33, concession A, Haldimand

dah, and the huge supporting beams provide evidence of its original appearance. The bake oven and fireplace are still intact.

A trim little red brick house between Grafton and Cobourg, south of the Danforth Road on lot 33, concession A, Haldimand, is a fine example of a Regency cottage – a style popular in the nineteenth century which is square in plan and has a shallow hipped roof extended to cover a verandah. In this house, a belvedere provides light to four bedrooms and a hall on the second floor. It was called Prospect Cottage, and was built by either Caleb Mallory or his son, Justis Friend Mallory, who inherited the property in 1847.

11

Cobourg

As in many of the lakeside towns, Cobourg's nineteenth century buildings are interspersed with younger neighbours. Still, it is surprising to find in a community this size such stately and grandiose early buildings as Victoria Hall and the equally impresive Victoria College. Throughout the town, as well, can be seen the mansions of the very rich – the homes of visiting Americans who, for over fifty years, added colour and excitement to the community. All these elements combine to give Cobourg an atmosphere entirely its own.

Where Cobourg stands today was once cedar swamp. As a result, the town was slower in becoming established than some of the adjacent centres along Lake Ontario. A few settlers had arrived, however, as early as 1798. Among them were four Burnham brothers, Asa, Zaccheus, John, and Mark, who with their sister Hannah emigrated from New Hampshire. In the ensuing years, the Burnhams became one of the most influential families in the area.

A two-storey frame house associated with the Burnhams stands on lot 18, concession 2, Hamilton, on the Danforth Road north of Cobourg. Two gravestones have been found there, dated 1812 and marking the burial places of infants. This would seem to indicate that a family was living on the property at the time. The present frame house, with its lovely old verandah and door, could have been built in that period, but it is difficult to determine the circumstances of its construction. We do know that Zaccheus Burnham bought the land in 1813 from the Crown grantee, Charles Shaw. We know also that at that time Zaccheus already had a home west of Cobourg. He must therefore have bought the land and house for some other reason, perhaps to provide accommodation for another member of the family. His children were young in 1813. But his brother Asa had just died, leaving a widow, Sarah Lovekin Burnham. Did Zaccheus buy the property on which Sarah was living to ensure her a home? In any event, by 1823 the assessment rolls showed Sarah living in a two-storey frame house on the property. This may well be the attractive, simple dwelling that is now being restored. On the road in front of it, some of the logs which made up the Danforth Road can be seen protruding through the surface.

Much of the land to the west of Cobourg was owned by Zaccheus Burnham. He was a public-spirited man – a militia officer in the War of 1812, a colonel during the Mackenzie Rebellion of 1837, a Member of the Legislative Assembly from 1834 to 1841. He built his neo-classic frame house, Whitehall (lot 22, concession 1, Hamilton), just west of the town, on land he had purchased in 1805. The house

Burnham house, lot 18, concession 2, Hamilton

has a finely designed porch protecting the front door, with well-proportioned windows on either side providing balance to the façade. It must be the 'frame house of two storeys with six additional fireplaces' referred to in the 1816 assessment rolls. Two years later, another fireplace had been added, possibly in a summer kitchen at the rear. Burnham and his wife, Elizabeth Choate, lived in the house until his death in 1856, when the property went to their son, Rev. Mark Burnham.

Another Burnham dwelling stands not far to the west (lot 25, concession 1) on land that was also owned initially by Zaccheus. The red brick house was built about 1865 by Asa Allworth Burnham for his son William, and has remained in the Burnham family until the present day. (Asa A. Burnham was mayor of Cobourg, an MLA, and a member of the first Senate of Canada.)

Along with the Burnham brothers, Eluid Nickerson shares the honour of being among the first settlers of Cobourg. Much of the

Whitehall, built by Zaccheus Burnham

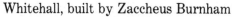

town was built on his original land grant. In 1816, Nickerson's son John sold fifty acres to young Ebenezer Perry, who had arrived in the village the previous year and stayed to become one of its most prominent citizens. Perry sold part of his property, now the southeast corner of King and Church Streets, to Robert Crosson in 1831. That same year the assessment rolls showed Crosson living in a frame house under two storeys in height. Whether he built it, or purchased it with the land, is uncertain, although the latter seems more likely. In 1833 the property was sold again, this time to Robert Henry, and in the assessment rolls for that year the dwelling is classed as two storeys, with five men and two women living in it. It seems likely that the east half of the present house was part of the first building, for that section has simple woodwork and low ceilings. When Henry expanded it later, he added the bay window as well as the western section.

Henry and his young wife shared the house with her brother, James Gray Bethune. (Norman Bethune, the Canadian doctor who became a hero in Spain and China, was a descendant.) Robert Henry had spent many years in the fur trade before settling in Cobourg, where he operated a flour mill, said to be one of the largest in Canada. He also ran a bank in the King Street house. The safe Henry used remained in the house for many years.

His brother-in-law, J.G. Bethune, also had banking interests and was involved in real estate. As an agent for the Canada Company, he was responsible for bringing many settlers to the Cobourg area. But he eventually went bankrupt, due to poor investments and a reach which exceeded his financial grasp.

Ebenezer Perry built the imposing red brick house at 420 Division Street. Perry had come from Ernestown after serving in the militia during the War of 1812. He later recalled that Cobourg was then nicknamed Hardscrabble, 'and hard scrabbling it was in 1815.' Perry prospered, however, acquiring large land holdings, a mill, a pork-packing plant, and a large general store. He acquired, as well, five wives. They were: Apphia Randolph, Ann Van Norman, Mrs Susanna Spencer, Susan Van Norman (Ann's sister), and Susan Bunestell.

The Perry house on Division Street dates from the 1850s. It was at one time flanked by one-storey wings built a few years after the main building. The wing on the north side burned down many years ago and was not replaced. An old brick coach house stands behind the main building.

During the 1830s Cobourg was a busy place. Catharine Parr Traill in *The Backwoods of Canada* described it as 'a neatly built and flourishing village, containing many good stores, mills, a banking-house [Robert Henry's] and printing office where a newspaper is published once a week. There is a very pretty church [Saint Peter's] and a select society, many families of respectability having fixed their residence in or near the town.' The newspaper to which she referred was the Cobourg *Star* which published its first issue on 11 January 1831. The *Star* is still being published, although the price is somewhat higher. A full year's subscription then was twelve shillings and six pence, just over three dollars.

Shortly before Mrs Traill wrote her description, the Methodists had begun construction of the Upper Canada Academy. The cornerstone was laid on 7 June 1832, but today no one knows which stone it

420 Division Street, the Ebenezer Perry house

was. The Academy was originally a grammar school, but in 1841 it extended its teaching to the university level and changed its name to Victoria College. The first president of the college was Rev. Egerton Ryerson, one of Canada's leading educators and then the outstanding Methodist in public life. The college was financed by contributions from across the province, and for fifty years was highly regarded academically. In 1890, Victoria federated with the University of Toronto and two years later moved to a new building in that city. In 1902, its original building became a provincial hospital. A majestic and imposing brick structure, it is seen in nearly every early sketch of the town, its cupola a landmark for miles. In one of W.H. Bartlett's most famous engravings of the 1840s, it dominates the landscape.

Of much smaller stature but even earlier date is the building at 128 Durham Street. It is said to have served as a storage shed during the War of 1812, but this has been impossible to confirm. In 1834

Methodist Upper Canada Academy, later Victoria College

it became a malt house for a local brewery and later a stables. It remains an attractive, simple structure – one of the few stone buildings in Cobourg.

At the south end of Tremaine Street is The Hill, a two-storey brick house (on lot 20, concession AB) with a prominent gable festooned with bargeboard. Built in 1836 for Winkworth Tremaine, a local merchant, it later became the home of William Weller, Upper Canada's leading stagecoach entrepreneur. Weller, who was born in Heinzburg, Vermont, arrived in Cobourg in the 1820s and in 1829 purchased the York-to-Kingston stagecoach line. Because of its reliability, Weller's business succeeded and gradually expanded until he dominated land travel in much of the province. It was no small achievement to carry passengers and mail with regularity over the rough highways of the period from Hamilton to Montreal, with branches to Dundas and Niagara, up Yonge Street and on many other routes.

Weller took pride in the design of his coaches, many of which were built in Cobourg. One of his passengers, Mrs William Radcliff, in writing to her husband in 1832, described a typical coach: 'Very showy and by no means ugly in appearance. There are three rows of seats in each; the centre seat moves on a pivot so as to clear the doorway and allow free ingress and egress, for those who occupy the other two ... Each seat holds four moderate persons, but three Radcliffs.' Weller also included in his coaches small desks made of rosewood or mahogany fitted with a pen rest and several drawers. It is difficult, however, to imagine how anyone could attempt to write while bouncing along the early Danforth Road.

In 1840 Weller demonstrated his enterprising spirit when, on a £1,000 bet, he drove his coach from Toronto to Montreal in 35 hours and 40 minutes. His passenger, Lord Sydenham, the governor-general, was anxious to catch a steamboat in Montreal and the record-breaking trip was made at a speed of nine miles per hour. Weller received £100 for the ride as well as the amount of the bet, a gold pocket watch, and a good deal of valuable publicity.

Weller served as mayor of Cobourg in 1850, 1851, and 1863. He was deeply involved in Cobourg's attempt to establish local supre-

The Hill, home of Winkworth Tremaine and later of William Weller of stagecoach fame

macy and acquired interests in the Cobourg and Peterborough Railroad. The railway failed, however, and Weller was forced to sell much of his property. He died a poor man in 1863 at the age of sixty-five. Weller's house later became the home of Nellie Sartoris, daughter of General Ulysses S. Grant of the United States. It is now a religious retreat.

During the period of mass immigration from the British Isles in the 1840s and 1850s, settlers arrived by the thousands in Upper Canada. Many came to Cobourg and then moved north, but others stayed and prospered. A number of the houses on King Street were built during this period. The John Field house at 323 King Street West is typical. It is a neat red brick house with a central gable, and French windows flanking the door. Field came from Somerset in 1834, and in the next year was running a general store in which presumably he lived (along with six other persons, according to the assessment rolls). The store apparently did well, for by 1839 he had

323 King Street West, home of John Field

moved to or built a two-storey frame house on a town lot (possibly 216 King Street West, still standing), and in 1847 he purchased his brick home. The house is built on bedrock. The kitchen was in the basement – a common location at the time.

In 1847, Field also bought the brick house at 212 King Street West. It eventually came to be known as the place where, in 1869, Marie Dressler was born. Her father was the organist of St Peter's Church, and she lived in the house for seventeen years before running away with a travelling opera troupe. By her twenties she was acting on Broadway with Lillian Russell. In 1907 she broke box office records in London, England. After that she financed a show which failed, leaving her $20,000 in debt. She returned to Broadway and Hollywood in 1914, acted with Charlie Chaplin, had a run-in with Florenz Ziegfield, retired, and married a promoter who spent all her money. Stardom returned in 1930 with a part in *Anna Christie*; twenty-four other films followed, the best known being

212 King Street West, known as the birthplace of Marie Dressler

Tugboat Annie. She died in 1934, leaving an estate of $280,000 and many devoted followers. They loved her for her talent, not her beauty – the little girl from Cobourg grew to be five feet ten inches tall and weighed over two hundred pounds.

Near the corner of King and Ontario streets, at 230 King Street West, is a two-storey brick house bought in 1854 by Thomas Scott, the postmaster. It was built as a storey-and-a-half dwelling with a verandah across the front, but has undergone changes since.

Cobourg's wealthy gravitated to the east end of town. Here on the north side of King Street the first Anglican church, St Peter's, was built in 1820. As the congregation grew so did the church. In 1829 nineteen feet were added to the north end and in 1833 side galleries were built. The tower was erected in 1844. The present brick church was built around and over the original frame building, which remained in use during the construction period that lasted until 1854.

Among the most prestigious nineteenth-century families in Cobourg were the Boultons. George Strange Boulton, born in the United States in 1797, was a lieutenant-colonel in the militia of Upper Canada and for twenty-six years a member of the Legislative Council. His large brick home at King and D'Arcy streets, Northumberland Hall, has been demolished.

Across the road from its site, however, at 201 D'Arcy Street, still stands the home of his nephew. D'Arcy Boulton was born in York at the family home, The Grange (now attached to the Art Gallery of Ontario), in 1814 and came to Cobourg in the 1830s, presumably at first living with his uncle in Northumberland Hall. He too was a lawyer, and uncle and nephew apparently were partners. D'Arcy married in 1838. His house, The Lawn, was built on part of a 150-acre Crown patent originally issued to George Boulton in 1839; D'Arcy became official owner in 1857. The south part of the house was built first. The Lawn is a gracious, well-proportioned building. A maple tree in front of it was planted by the Prince of Wales when he was a guest of the Boultons during a visit to Cobourg in 1860.

George Boulton's Crown grant embraced the block bounded by Chapel, D'Arcy, Henry, and James streets, and included the gabled brick house at 308 Henry Street. The first floor and basement of this house are early in date. By 1857 the east wall was already so weathered that it needed repairs, and the man who did the work carved his name – Thos. H. Bradbeer – along with the date in the soft brick. If we may assume that it would take more than twenty years for the thick hand-made brick to weather badly, then the first part of the building may well have pre-dated the official Crown grant. In 1865 the property passed by quitclaim from George to his daughter, Harriet; but the house's builder is unknown.

A fine peaked gable and excellent brickwork are features of the John Cullingford house at the southwest corner of George and Havelock Streets. Cullingford bought the property in 1856 and the house was probably built shortly after that. *The Northumberland and Durham Directory for 1860* shows Cullingford running a drugstore on George street. He was still in business when *Dodd's Directory* appeared in 1880.

Yet another beautiful small building in north Cobourg is 411 John Street. William Hitchins, a grocer, owned it in 1860. Fine windows are deeply recessed on the second level. The staircase, baseboards, and other interior woodwork are skilfully carved.

308 Henry Street

North of the town, at the northeast corner of Elgin and Ontario streets, stands Pratt's Mill and a small mill house overlooking the mill pond. This property was originally held by Asa Burnham, who sold it to Ebenezer Perry in 1836 for £150. Perry's mill was of stone, but it burned and was replaced with a brick structure. The mill came into the Pratt family in 1889 and has been operated by the same family ever since. It was almost destroyed by another fire in 1942, but the structure was saved and the brick walls are still those erected by Perry.

Cobourg's main street is dominated by Victoria Hall, designed by the well-known Toronto architect of the mid-nineteenth century, Kivas Tulley, and opened in 1860 by the Prince of Wales. It is considered one of the finest classical revival buildings in Ontario. Behind the massive portico and under the cupola, the central block houses the court room and council chamber on the first floor, and a

Pratt's Mill, Elgin and Ontario Streets

Home of John Cullingford, George and Havelock Streets

Grand Concert Hall on the second. The exterior is faced with free-stone on all but the rear portion, which is brick. Victoria Hall took four years to build. It was conceived as a symbol of Cobourg's ambitions, but not long afterward the fortunes of the town began to decline. The building could not be kept up, but in the 1970s a major restoration was undertaken to return the main rooms to past splendour.

Other houses in Cobourg of historical interest include the Anglican Church School at 117 King Street East, built in the 1830s; the home of Senator William Kerr at 272 King Street, built in the 1840s; The Poplars on Spencer Street East, built in 1828 by John Spencer; and the Church of England Diocesan Theological College at 174 Green Street, built in the 1840s. The last-mentioned was once known as the Corktown School – Corktown and Kerrytown were the areas in which Irish immigrants to Cobourg settled. In one year alone, 1847, 'the black year of emigration,' more than 5,000 Irish-

Victoria Hall, opened by the Prince of Wales in 1860

men, many sick from typhus and cholera, landed in Cobourg and other lake ports. Many had paid the passage to Toronto, but were dropped by ships' captains anxious to be rid of the infection.

No description of Cobourg is complete without mention of happier arrivals – 'The Americans.' For over fifty years the town was the summer home of dozens of families who came up from the United States for the air, with the idea that Cobourg's 'ozone' was the best on the continent. This influx began about 1870, and by the turn of the century the town was the 'Newport of the North,' the location of ornate mansions built by the steel magnates of Pittsburgh and their associates. The visitors came for six months of the year, bringing servants, guests, and a style of life that thrived on frequent and lavish entertaining. Katherine Cornell was married in the house at 139 Queen Street in 1922. Sidbrook, on King Street East, was the home of the Abbotts of Pittsburgh. The George Howes of Pittsburgh lived on the same street. It all ended with the crash of 1929

Ravensworth, Lake Ontario summer home of General Fitzhugh

and the depression that followed. Since then many of the mansions have been torn down or burned. Some have become public buildings.

The American houses are newer than others we have mentioned, but they changed the character of Cobourg. Of those still standing, one of the most magnificent is Ravensworth, on the shore of Lake Ontario just east of the town. Built in 1900, it was the summer home of General Fitzhugh, a Virginian who fought for the Union during the Civil War and married into a Pennsylvania steel-making family. The house, built for entertaining, has spacious rooms and high ceilings. The interior detailing throughout is ornate and lavish. In the dining room – where dinner parties for twenty or thirty were common – the walls are covered with French tapestries. A broad staircase leads to the many bedrooms on the second floor. With its columned porticoes, curving driveway, and well-manicured lawn stretching down to the lake, Ravensworth would not look out of place in the Deep South. On Lake Ontario, it is a reminder of a romantic but almost forgotten past.

12

Port Hope

The first Crown grants issued in a new settlement did not necessarily go to the families who were the first to occupy the land. Certain conditions had to be met regarding clearing the acreage before a patent could be approved. In addition, some connection with those in power was a distinct advantage. The first patents in Smith's Creek went to Captain Jonathan Walton and Elias Smith in 1797. They received the whole site of what was later Port Hope, even though a number of settlers had been on the land since 1793. One of these was Lawrence Herkimer, brother of Nicholas Herkimer of Herkimer's Nose near Kingston; a fur trader, he had built a log house and was engaged in a successful business until he lost the land to Walton.

Elias Smith and his wife Catherine came to Upper Canada from Orange County, New York. By 1795 Elias had built a mill with the assistance of Joseph Keeler, Colborne's first settler. The Smiths were accompanied by some of their ten children, among them John David, who built The Bluestone in 1834. This magnificent building, at 21 Dorset Street East, is one of the finest examples of the classical revival style in Ontario.

John David Smith served as a captain in the War of 1812, and later as a member of the Legislative Assembly. The Bluestone was a wedding gift to his second wife, Augusta Louisa Woodward. The Smiths undoubtedly needed all the room that the spacious house afforded, for eventually there were fourteen children – ten born to John David's first wife Susan, and four to Augusta Louisa. As in the Allan Macpherson house in Napanee, the front and rear façades of The Bluestone are identical. Stone for the foundation came from the nearby Ganaraska River. For the remainder, large limestone blocks were transported to the site from Kingston. Stucco now covers the stone. The house's name referred either to the colour of the limestone or to the colour of paint applied to the stucco, a shade then called stone-blue. The house is rich in architectural detailing, much more so than most built in the province at the time. Skilled craftsmen from England and the Continent were hired to carve the interior mouldings and create the ornate plaster ceilings. A cargo of Italian marble is said to have been lost in Lake Ontario on its way to Port Hope for The Bluestone's nine mantelpieces.

Elias Smith and Jonathan Walton donated the land on which St Mark's, the Anglican church on King Street, was built. Walton also donated a bell that is still in use. The church, initially called St John the Evangelist, was built in 1822. Sometime before 1851 the spire was added and other changes and additions made. A new Anglican

The Bluestone, 21 Dorset Street East

church was built across the river in 1869 and the little white church was closed. One of the church wardens, not wanting the Walton bell to ring in any other building, buried it in a nearby field; the bell was unearthed when St Mark's re-opened four years later. Inside the church, the simplicity of the hand-hewn beams and the early box pews blends pleasantly with later additions – the altar, triptych, and chancel. Many of the town's first settlers are buried in the church cemetery. So is the first Canadian-born governor-general, Rt. Hon. Vincent Massey.

For many years the small settlement was known as Smith's Creek, not after Elias but Peter Smith, a fur trader who had a post on the east side of the creek, opposite the present town hall, as early as 1778. It was he who made the disputed sale of land to Nicholas Herkimer. When the first post office opened in 1817, an official name had to be chosen. For a while the village had been called Toronto, but this name was also set aside, to be picked up in 1834 by a growing community some sixty miles to the west. Port Hope was chosen instead.

Port Hope grew prosperous. The harbour bustled with activity. Exports of agricultural products, lumber, and internationally famous whiskey left the docks daily. During the 1830s, as many as fifty vessels docked in one week.

Captain Wallace owned a schooner, a wharf, and a lumber exporting business. The low frame building that stands at the south end of King Street is thought to have been built for him. Later it became the Seaman's Inn and later still a girls' boarding school. The third floor contains a series of small rooms which could have accommodated, successively, Wallace's nine children, lake sailors, and finally young students. The house fell into disrepair, but in recent years the ugly insulbrick facing has been removed, revealing the pleasant frame structure underneath. The Wallace home is now known as Canada House. Near it on King Street stand several modest frame houses which for many years were occupied by other lake captains.

Most of the buildings on Walton Street, Port Hope's main street, were built in the 1850s, and this partially explains the coherence of architectural styles. To maintain a horizontal roof line in spite of the slope of the hill took some ingenuity, and sills and frames had to be adjusted at the lower levels. Many of the buildings at the west end of the street are residential, but they blend well with the commercial structures, even repeating some classical details, as in the terraced house at 134–6 Walton Street. Perhaps the finest building on the street is the St Lawrence Hotel with its Italianate façade.

Two of Walton Street's early buildings, although of little architectural interest, were involved in the career of one of Port Hope's most remarkable citizens – William Hunt, later known as Signor Gilnor Gilarma Farini or 'Farini the Great.' He was one of the most amazing men produced in Canada during the last century, and it is surprising that so little is known of him today.

William Hunt was born in Lockport, New York, but his family moved to Bowmanville and then to Port Hope when he was a small child. He studied medicine for a short time, until one day he saw a tightrope act at a visiting circus. Hunt was captivated and practised the art. He made his first public appearance in Port Hope in 1859. Two years later, after spectacular feats elsewhere, he returned to his home town to walk – with peach baskets on his feet – on a rope stretched between the Waddell Block (at the southeast corner of Walton and Mill) and the Gillett Building (at the southeast corner of Walton and Queen): there were then no buildings between these two. The stunt was a great success, but Hunt's father felt the family had been disgraced, and the young man left home.

Between these two appearances in Port Hope, he performed at Niagara Falls, and not as William Hunt but under the more theatrical name of Farini. He was about twenty years old, but repeated all the tricks of the much more famous Blondin – then at the height of popularity – even adding a few of his own. To the delight of the ever-increasing crowds, Farini climbed down to the *Maid of the Mists* from the centre of a slack rope strung across the gorge, then ascended to the cable again; he cooked a meal over the falls while on a rope; he walked on sixteen-foot stilts through the water at the head of the falls. Not satisfied with the title of aerialist, he dubbed himself a 'pangymnastikonaerostationist.' Up to ten thousand people flocked to see him perform, and several excursion trains carried fans from Port Hope, Colborne, and Cobourg.

Farini was not unaware of the value of publicity. In August 1860, when the Prince of Wales visited Canada and watched Blondin perform, Farini offered to

take the heir apparent to the British throne across the falls in a wheelbar-

St Lawrence Hotel, Walton Street

row, on a tightrope, free of expense. In this way thousands may see him who would not have an opportunity if he came by railroad or any ordinary conveyance. The greatest natural phenomenon on this continent has been running over six thousand years in preparation for this event.

The prince did not take up the offer. But there is a story, often repeated, that Farini pushed his wife in a wheelbarrow on a tightrope across the Falls – and dropped her when he stopped to wave at some fans. The Niagara Falls *Gazette* in December 1862 reported a variation on this story of 'the death of Farini's wife due to a fall from his back at the Plaza Torres Bull Ring, in Havana, Cuba.' But Farini kept a diary for much of his life, and a search through eight volumes of his papers has turned up no evidence that he was married at this point.

Farini did marry at the age of forty-six. He chose for his bride Anna Muller, a concert pianist who was the daughter of an aide-de-camp to the German Kaiser, a niece of Richard Wagner, and a former pupil of Franz Liszt. The couple had one son, Willie Leonard Farini.

During the first world war, they were detained in Germany and forced to act as interpreters. Farini wrote a history of the war that filled thirty-six notebooks. His other writings indicate the breadth of his interests and travel: they include *Through the Kalahari, Ferns Which Grow in New Zealand*, and articles on 'How to make Yogurt,' 'The Devil,' and 'Ladies' Hats.' Farini was also an inventor (with forty patents to his credit), a sculptor, and a painter. In 1908, his paintings were exhibited in Toronto with those of C.W. Jefferys. He travelled to many parts of the world but returned to Port Hope. He died in 1929.

To the north of Port Hope, west of the village of Welcome, is the red brick house where William Farini Hunt grew up. It is located on lot 22, concession 3, Hope, on the first concession road north of Highway 2. In later years, Hunt purchased part of lot 21, just east of the original homestead. The small brick stable where he reputedly practised for his first aerial act is still standing at the south end of lot 22, beside Highway 2, the Danforth Road. In 1889 he made his last move, to the William Marsh farm, lot 17, concession 2, Hope.

A singular feature of Port Hope architecture is the presence of many small 'Ontario cottages' in which classical details have been finely applied in a scale appropriate to the buildings' size. The Trick house, at 254 Ridout Street, is a good example, It was built on part of a Crown grant made in 1832 to Thomas Gibbs Ridout, who held the land until the 1850s when it was subdivided and sold. Richard Trick, a mason, bought this lot in 1850 and likely built the house shortly afterwards. The main floor is several feet above grade level because the original kitchen was in the basement and required windows. The house remained in the family for seventy-one years. *Dodds' Directory* of 1880 lists a descendant of Richard as owning the 'J. Trick Planing Mill and Well Tube Factory' which was located in Barrett's Block on Cavan Street. For many years the Trick house was a store. The owner kept black walnuts in a basket on his verandah, and squirrels would get into them. Today the verandah has disappeared, but the squirrels have left a legacy – a number of splendid walnut trees.

The cottage at 284 Ridout Street shows elements of classical revival in the heavy pilasters at either end of the façade and the

Home of 'Farini' Hunt, lot 22, concession 3, Hope

slightly detached fan transom. The date of construction, 1850, appears over the door. In that year the property, another part of the Ridout block, was sold to Thomas Spry, a local blacksmith. He was still living there in 1880.

Thomas Gibbs Ridout, who sold both properties, had come to Upper Canada as a youth at the end of the Revolutionary War, and at the age of nineteen had been appointed deputy assistant commissary general, possibly owing to the fact that his father, Thomas Sr, was surveyor-general at the time. From 1822 to 1861 he was cashier (a position equivalent to general manager) of the Bank of Upper Canada. The Port Hope property was chiefly an investment, but nevertheless many of the town's streets were named after his family: Charles Street after his son, Julia Street after his daughter Juliana, and Dorset Street after the English county from which the Ridouts came.

Among many other 'Ontario cottages,' three stand out: The Bel-

Richard Trick house, 254 Ridout Street

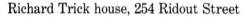

vedere at 95 Augusta Street, 15 Julia Street, and the cottage at the end of Little Hope Street. All show much attention to detail and quality of workmanship.

Port Hope is also fortunate in possessing attractive row housing. Barrett's Terrace which joins Cavan Street and Ontario Street is one example. The builder successfully avoided monotony along the façade by imaginative use of low-relief brick work and by repetition of a lyre motif on the verandah posts. Other examples can be found throughout the town.

An architectural feature frequently seen on Port Hope buildings is a decorative trim known as 'cresting.' This ornate ironwork was a product of the Helm foundry, a firm operated by one of the town's earliest families. The foundry was located in the town centre. The family home – now the Greenwood Towers – was on the Danforth Road east of the town. It was built in 1866. A handsome water tower was built next to it nine years later. The tower has good windows,

Pinehurst, Nesbitt Kirchhoffer's Pine Street home

artistic wrought iron, and ornate brick work, all unusual in such a utilitarian structure.

At 44 Pine Street North, on a lot that once contained over one hundred pine trees, stands a house with the appropriate name of Pinehurst. It was built in 1846 by Nesbitt Kirchhoffer, who had been practising law in Port Hope since 1840. (He was an uncle of Senator John Nesbitt Kirchhoffer.) In 1890 the house was sold to a descendant of Elias Smith. The new owners' daughter recalled her mother's initial reaction to the house: 'I wouldn't have Pinehurst as a gift.' This was probably because Ada Kirchhoffer always kept the shutters closed, and the house impressed Mrs Smith as being 'a dismal, dark, and musty mansion.' Mr Smith nevertheless bought it for $5,000 over his wife's objections. In her memoirs, their daughter described Pinehurst:

It is not a spacious house but the buttresses on the corners make it appear larger than it really is. There are French windows opening into the rooms and in my time during the summers they stood open. On the ground floor we had sitting, drawing and dining rooms, these with open fireplaces. Around three sides of the house were terraces flanked by brick walls with stone steps leading down to lower lawns. We had a coal furnace with no pipe leading upstairs, so Mother had a small box-stove named Black Beauty in her bedroom and around which on chilly mornings we made our toilet. In the kitchen was a force pump and in the unfinished attic, a storage tank. The pump had to be serviced by hand and it required 50 hearty strokes to raise the water 1 inch. Here our 'boy friends' worked many a week for their Sunday supper after church.

From the west end of Ridout Street and south to Lake Ontario once lay the property of the Williams family. Here in 1828 John Tucker Williams built his home and called it Penryn, after his ancestral home in Cornwall.

Williams served under Lord Nelson and came to Canada during the War of 1812. He took part in that war and later commanded the Durham Regiment during the Rebellion of 1837. From 1841 to 1848 he sat as a Member of Parliament. Political campaigns in those days were never dull. Williams' opponent in the election of 1843 was George Strange Boulton of Cobourg. The followers of both resorted to rioting. One man was killed during one of many clashes between the two factions. Because of the difficulty of travel, voting stretched over six days, and on the last day, with Williams ahead, the opposition threatened to tear down the polling booth and remove the poll-books. Williams won, however.

His son, Arthur T. Williams, built an impressive home just to the west of Penryn when he married Emily Seymour. Called Penryn Park, it has recently been converted into a private club. In 1900 a billiard house was built immediately behind it. Arthur Williams was the lieutenant-colonel commanding the 46th battalion of volunteer militia sent against Louis Riel during the North West Rebellion of 1885. Port Hope was proud of him and his troops, and each man was given $100 by Mayor Ward 'for the purchase of extra underwear and other equipment.' Williams – the 'hero of Batoche' – led his battalion to victory, an event which was re-enacted at home by jubilant townspeople, some dressed as Indians and Métis rebels. But soon after the battle, still in the North West, Colonel Williams died. His triumphal return became a funeral procession with fifteen thousand

Penryn Park, built for Arthur Williams, the 'hero of Batoche'

people in attendance. A statue of him in front of the town hall was unveiled in 1889 by Sir John A. Macdonald.

During his visit on that occasion to Port Hope, the prime minister spent the night at the home of H.A. Ward, Member of Parliament for East Durham. He also visited Dunain (from the Gaelic Duncwm, 'Hill of the Birds'). This imposing house, at 345 Lakeshore Road, belonged to William Fraser, whose family home near the River Ness in Scotland inspired its name. The land on which it was built was part of the Williams property and the house was a gift from her brother to Augusta Williams when she married Fraser in 1857. Fraser had come to Port Hope eleven years earlier as the representative of a group of Montreal merchants, and had since become manager of the Commercial Bank at Cavan and Walton Streets.

Augusta Fraser was a talented singer and a noted beauty. Married at the age of twenty, she had borne five children by the time she

Dunain, 345 Lakeshore Road

was twenty-five. It did not seem to affect her looks. In 1860 she attended a ball in Montreal in honour of the Prince of Wales, and danced with the future king after he asked – according to family history – to meet 'the young lady with the lovely arms and neck.' One of her daughters married Frederic Barlow Cumberland, who became general manager of the Niagara Steamship Lines. Over the front door at Dunain is a stained glass window that came originally from the captain's cabin on the steamship *Cumberland*. (Frederic's father, F.W. Cumberland, was a well-known architect who designed University College and the façade of Osgoode Hall in Toronto.)

At Trafalgar and Victoria Streets is a large villa of the Italianate style that was popular in the 1860s. Idalia was built for a sister of Colonel Williams, Mrs Charles Seymour. Asymmetrical in plan, it boasts a balconied tower, ornate roof brackets, and a turret with a pointed, dome-shaped roof – a later addition.

Port Hope was obviously prospering during the 1850s and '60s,

Idalia, Trafalgar and Victoria Streets

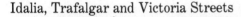

for other villas were rising at that time. The Port Hope *Guide* of 25 September 1858 described The Cone at 115 Dorset Street as one which 'promises to be, when completed, a veritable Gem.' This was the home of Thomas Curtis Clark, a merchant and associate engineer for the Port Hope, Lindsay and Beaverton Railway. His wife was Elias Smith's daughter Susan. Twenty years later J.G. 'Yankee' Williams, who bought the house in 1874, added the eastern half, containing a dining room and bedrooms. He was called 'Yankee' Williams to distinguish him from the local Williams family.

North of Port Hope, in an amazingly sylvan setting considering its proximity to Highway 401, is a mill and a small house that belonged to the Molson family. The property was granted to Jonathan Walton in 1804, sold by him to Zaccheus Burnham of Cobourg in 1817, and then (with one owner in between) to Horace Perry in 1831. In his will Perry mentioned a 'dwelling house and out buildings'; it seems likely that this trim storey-and-a-half frame house was the dwelling to which he referred. Certainly its architectural detailing relates to the period.

In 1855 Thomas Molson bought the site for £337 and the mill was probably built shortly afterward. Molson had broken away from his family's Montreal brewing interests and had established himself in Kingston and Port Hope. The distillery he opened was one of several (eight at one point) that produced Port Hope whiskey, a local product made with the waters of the Ganaraska that was famous in Europe for much of the nineteenth century. Molson's resident manager was Robert Orr, and it was probably he who occupied the mill house. In a history of the Molsons, Merrill Denison reported that correspondence with Orr indicated holdings in Port Hope that included one, and probably two distilleries, a brewery, saw, flour, and grist mills, at least one stave factory, one or more warehouses, and what was then the best wharf in the harbour.

At the west end of Port Hope stands the home of John Brand, a farmer. He built the red brick house at 350 Lakeshore Road sometime between 1855 and 1865. It is a handsome building, exemplifying those characteristics that made this style so popular in Ontario. The peaked gable, graceful cathedral window, and delicate bargeboard are beautifully proportioned and executed. The property (lot 10, concession 1, Hope Township) was purchased from John Shuter

The Molson mill, beside Highway 401

Smith, Brand's neighbour to the west, and the house was built for Brand by his father, Daniel Brand, whose homestead was further along the Lakeshore Road. The house remains today in its original condition. To some extent this may be due to the fact that John Brand's wife was a meticulous housekeeper, so much so, it is said, that few of the family or friends were ever invited inside lest they disturb its perfection. Subsequent owners have treasured its happy state.

Next door, at 366 Lakeshore Road, is Wildwood, the home of John Shuter Smith. He was a grandson of Elias Smith and served as a Member of Parliament from 1857 to 1864. He is said to have addressed his constituents from a balcony on the east side of the house. In the early part of this century, racing stables and a track were located at the rear. There is a sad family story about John Shuter's wife, Josephine Jones. After the death of her husband, Josephine married a German count and left with him to live in his

John Brand house, 350 Lakeshore Road

castle in Europe. After some years abroad, during which time she had been receiving interest from her inheritance, she wrote demanding the principal. Her brothers-in-law became suspicious and set out to investigate. They found the count's castle, and Josephine incarcerated within it. After that, Josephine went home to Port Hope. Josephine's great-niece, Phyllis M. Smith, told this story in her memoirs (kept in Port Hope). She added a detail which might have warned the family. The count had given his bride, as a wedding present, a gold locket with his family arms and his initials both set into it in pearls. 'Josephine,' remarked Phyllis Smith, 'must have been horrified on receiving the bill for it.'

West on the Lakeshore Road, on lot 15, concession 1, Hope, is a two-storey brick house that belonged to Daniel Brand. The Crown grant for the land was a late one, issued jointly in 1842 and 1845 to Brand and his father-in-law. Daniel Brand was born in 1792 in Ipswich, England. After settling in Canada, he made numerous trips

John Shuter Smith's Wildwood, 366 Lakeshore Road

back to England in connection with an inheritance, the receipt of which undoubtedly made his life as a farmer in Canada more comfortable. The brick on the Brand house, which covers the earlier frame structure, was laid by Richard Trick, the mason on Ridout Street.

The Lakeshore Road from Port Hope to Newcastle can rightly be called a heritage highway, for it was completed in 1800, making it one of the first roads in Upper Canada. During the War of 1812 it was used as a military road. For many years after, cannon balls were found in the adjacent fields where they had been stored. An older resident in the area recalls a tale passed down through generations, of a small boy who never forgot the sight of the sun glinting on the soldiers' bayonets.

During the war the authorities concluded that this road, situated so close to the lake, was vulnerable to attack. A new road was built to the north, on the third concession, and was opened in 1817.

To the west of Port Hope, the Lakeshore Road passes through Port Britain, a community that was, in mid-century, equal in size and prosperity to neighbouring Port Hope. Today only a handful of houses remain. Port Britain's prosperity was the result of the energy of one family, that of Samuel Marsh and his descendants. At its peak, Port Britain exported over two hundred masts per year for the Royal Navy, and sent lumber across the sea on the sailings ships of the Marsh Line.

The history of Port Britain begins in Manchester, Vermont, where William Marsh chose to remain loyal to the Crown and eventually left with his family to take up land in Canada. William received amnesty after the war and returned to Vermont, where he is said to have searched in vain for the family silver and pewter his wife had hidden from the rebels in their farm pond: the pond had a quicksand bottom. His sons remained in Canada.

According to another family story, William's sons were passing through Carrying Place on the Bay of Quinte when they saw some young ladies skating on a pond. Samuel Marsh took one look at young Jane Ostrum, pulled his horse to a halt, and announced that he had just seen his future wife. In February of that winter they were married, and a year later moved to Port Britain where they built a log house in 1796. Samuel Marsh died of ague (a malarial fever) in 1813, leaving nine children, the oldest of whom was William, then aged sixteen. It was William who created the vast lumbering and shipping business.

On the north side of Highway 2, west of Welcome (on lot 19, concession 3, Hope), stands the house that William built in 1825. It was associated with a stage coach inn; guests were housed in an east wing that contained a tavern, driving shed, stables, and a ballroom. The house had eight large rooms, each with a fireplace. A deer park was located on the property.

A strange request from William's sister, Susannah, prompted the building of a Marsh family vault that still can be seen near Lake Ontario. Susannah wanted a marble tomb, and on her death she became the twenty-seventh and last member to be placed inside it.

Just east of the creek in Port Britain (lot 20, concession 1) is a sturdy stone house that was built for William's brother Robert. Both the house and barn were built before 1850. The house seems to have been planned in a somewhat haphazard fashion, for no one window is located directly over another. The most interesting feature of this small building is a signature scratched carefully in the glass: 'R.B. Marsh, 1856.'

William Marsh inn and home, lot 19, concession 3, Hope

Set well back from the road, on the west side of the creek (lot 21, concession 1, Hope) is the home of Joseph Major, a miller. The house, stucco over frame, was built shortly before 1848. The community then supported more than three hundred and fifty people, including one wagonmaker, two blacksmiths, two coopers, two shopkeepers, two builders, a stonemason, contractor, station master, harbourmaster, postmaster, teacher, veterinarian, innkeeper, fishermen, and a tailor, not to speak of those involved in William Marsh's shipping and lumbering business. Today there is little to indicate that Port Britain was once such an active and prosperous village. The Marsh family, however, is still represented, for the miller's house is owned by a direct descendant of Samuel Marsh, keeping ties with the community that go back nearly two hundred years.

Tanglewood Farms lies further west along the Lakeshore Road on lot 11, Broken Front concession, Clarke. There, standing by the

Log house, on the Lakeshore Road, lot 11 Broken Front concession, Clarke

shore of the lake, is a small log house looking just as it did one hundred and fifty years ago. It was built on land that belonged to King's College until 1850 but the house was certainly there long before that. Some details of the construction suggest a date in the 1820s, and a small scrap of wallpaper found in one of the bedrooms has a pattern used extensively in New England at that time. One architectural historian feels that this fine log building may well have been constructed by shipwrights. Inside, a narrow staircase winds up behind the massive fireplace to two small bedrooms. The doors, which retain their original hardware, are made of solid pine slabs, twenty-six inches wide.

In 1855, Andrew Thomas purchased the house and land from the University of Toronto (the successor to King's College) and farmed it for about forty years. His name last appears on the title in 1896. Eleven years later, William Thomas (perhaps a son) sold the property to Alfred and Percy Brown. For a long time after this, the small log house was used as a sheep barn. Recent owners have lovingly and authentically restored it.

13

Newcastle

Except for the few people who settled along the lakeshore, Darlington and Clarke Townships were largely unpopulated until sometime after 1830 – not because no one wanted the land, but because some Crown grants were held for speculation. This situation lasted until a tax on wild land was made permanent in 1823. After that many owners sold their property.

This is probably the reason why William Jarvis sold his two hundred-acre lot in Clarke Township (lot 5, concession 1) in 1824. The property was bought by George Beard for £50. It was sold thirty years later by Joshua George Beard to Joseph Thompson for £200. Whether or not the stone house now on the property was included in the sale is uncertain. If not, it was built by Thompson shortly after the purchase; a mortgage he took out in 1860 may be a clue. The stone of the house varies from pink to grey.

Joshua George Beard was no longer living on the property when he sold it. He had moved by 1848 to Toronto, where he had a hostelry at Church and Colborne streets and an iron foundry. In 1854 he was elected mayor of the city; among his responsibilities in office was removal of the sheds built to house cholera victims. He was an impressive-looking man – bald, but with a flowing beard and moustache.

Along the road to the west in Newtonville (lot 8, concession 1, Clarke) is another small stone house. It was built by an Irishman named Humphrey Jones who, with his widowed mother and four brothers, settled in Canada in 1820. Local records suggest that he built his house in 1835. He did not, however, receive his Crown grant until twelve years later, a fact which casts some doubt on the earlier date. In any case the house is in fine condition today, in large measure because it has remained in the family. Six generations of Joneses have cared for it over the years.

Hugh Ovens was another Irish immigrant who came with his family to settle in Clarke Township. They arrived about the middle of the century, and in 1854 Hugh got married and purchased a farm (lot 11, concession 1). Like the Joneses, the Ovenses have been living there ever since. The house has been altered. The barn is of interest because it has weathered the years so well: few early barns in the area remain in such good condition.

When Daniel Massey left the Grafton-Cobourg area and arrived in Newcastle in 1847, that village was a growing, spirited community with a busy harbour. Increased traffic along the Danforth Road had created a need for innkeepers and tradesmen to cater to the stage coaches that rolled by every day. Blacksmiths, wagonmakers

George Beard house, lot 5, concession 1, Clarke

and saddlers were doing a brisk business. It was here that Massey established the Newcastle Foundry and Machine Manufactory, a small concern that grew to become the giant Massey-Ferguson Limited. Daniel Massey founded, as well, a family renowned for its generosity and for its contributions to Canada's political and cultural life.

Not long after the Masseys settled in Newcastle, they built a spacious cobblestone house at 285 Mill Street. Although the older children were grown and on their own, there were still three daughters and a son at home. Another daughter was born shortly after they arrived.

In 1851, Hart Massey joined his father in the family business. His salary was four hundred dollars per year. Hart's children loved to visit 'the old homestead,' as Daniel's house was always called. Every Christmas there was a joyous family gathering there, with the grandchildren marching noisily around the yard and wide extensive verandahs, blowing fifes and banging drums. (One of the grandchildren was Chester, father of Vincent and Raymond Massey.) Today the verandahs are gone and the cobblestones have been covered with brick. The mansard roof is a later addition as well.

Daniel Massey died intestate in 1856. His property was later divided between his son Hart and daughters Arletta and Alida (then aged thirteen and nine). Hart and his family moved into 'the old homestead' in 1870 and lived there for two years. The house was then sold to Rev. Henry Brent, the first rector of the Anglican church across the road.

Henry Brent began his ministry in the same year that Daniel Massey started the Newcastle foundry. He was appointed to act as a travelling missionary in the Newcastle and Colborne districts, an area stretching roughly from Lake Ontario to Lake Nipissing. Given the condition of the roads at the time, this must have been quite a challenge and Brent did encounter difficulties. In a letter to Rev. William Herchimer the following year, Bishop Strachan remarked 'something will have to be done' for Brent. What, if anything, was done we don't know, but Brent continued with his work and in 1857 became rector of the newly built St George's Church, diagonally across from the Massey house. He remained as rector until his death forty-one years later. Brent's house is now the rec-

The Ovens barn, lot 11, concession 1, Clarke

tory of St George's, as it has been since it was bought by the Diocese of Toronto in 1896.

Immediately to the north of the Massey-Brent house, at 261 Mill Street, is a tall, gothic-style structure, replete with fanciful bargeboard and intricately carved exterior wood trim. This was the home of W.T. Boate, the county school superintendant. His refined and spacious residence suggests that either Boate or his wife had a private income, for the house contained six fireplaces, servants' quarters, and an elegant carriage house. It was built before 1861.

Within a few years of moving into their magnificent new home, the Boates were struck by tragedy. Two children died suddenly. The *Canadian Statesman* of 13 November 1862 reported that three-year-old Mary Rosalie had died of scarlet fever two days earlier and – in a style typical of the period – remarked: 'As this is the second bereavement which Mr Boate has had to suffer, having lost his only son about 6 weeks ago, he has the warmest sympathies of a

The former Massey homestead, 285 Mill Street

large circle of friends.' One would like to think that Mrs Boate had their sympathy as well.

In 1859, about the time the Boate house was going up, a more modest frame house was constructed a few blocks away at 102 Church Street. It was built by Hart Massey as a parsonage for the Methodist Church. The Masseys were staunch Methodists and for many years Hart taught Sunday School in the local church where young Chester played the organ. Originally the house had no second storey on the south side. The verandah too is a later addition. The house is in excellent condition, and the present owners are restoring it carefully.

To the north of the parsonage, on King Street (Highway 2) just west of Baldwin Street, is another good-looking frame house, The Hollows. The front part was not built until the turn of the century, but has been tastefully restored. The rear sections of the building are of an early date and part at the far back may well be a product

261 Mill Street, home of W.T. Boate

of the 1830s. The central section appears to be of 1870 vintage. The land title provides no clues to the builder of the house, but the property was owned originally by Captain John McGill, who sold it in 1801 to Robert Baldwin, one of the township's first settlers and grandfather of Hon. Robert Baldwin, Reform statesman and twice joint premier of the Province of Canada in the 1840s.

Also on King Street, on the east side of the village, is a white frame house that is now the office of the Newcastle *Reporter*. For many years the property belonged to the Wallbridge family.

Asa Wallbridge arrived in Newcastle in 1816 and purchased the north half of lot 27, concession 1. He was the son of one of the early settlers in Prince Edward County and a nephew of the Asa Wallbridge who built the first house in Belleville. In 1853 he took out a mortgage for £44, and it was probably then that he built the small cottage on the property. Within a few months he sold it to his son Elijah. Asa was seventy-two years old, and no doubt glad to have his

102 Church Street, built as the Methodist parsonage

son living nearby. He died six years later. His own home stands to the east of the small house he built for his son.

Local sources suggest that, in later years, Elijah Wallbridge's home was bought by Joseph E. Atkinson as a residence for his sister. Atkinson, who became publisher of the Toronto *Star*, was born and grew up in Newcastle. He was only six months old when his father died, and to support herself and eight children his mother ran a boarding house for workers of the Massey's iron foundry. Her struggles and the years of poverty the family endured resulted in Joe Atkinson's life-long concern for the underdog.

The Massey factory still is in commercial use in Newcastle, at the corner of King and Beaver Streets. A very ordinary, three-storey brick building, it was put up in 1864 after the original structure was destroyed by fire. In 1879 the Massey company moved to Toronto but its factory, the 'old homestead,' the Methodist Church, and the parsonage all remain – lasting reminders of a remarkable family.

Elijah Wallbridge's home, King Street

14

Bowmanville

Of the many types of architecture that developed in pre-Confederation Canada, the most unusual by far was the polygonal building. Throughout Ontario this style was hastily and enthusiastically embraced during the 1840s and '50s for houses, barns, jails, and even privies. Bowmanville has one of the better examples. Although it is not a particularly handsome house, the octagon at 48 Division Street is in excellent repair, and no one has tried to modernize it.

The fad for octagonal buildings was due, in part, to the influence of an eccentric American named Orson Squire Fowler. He was a man of many interests who wrote on subjects ranging from phrenology to sex. One of his books, *Amativeness: or, Evils and Remedies of Excessive and Perverted Sexuality, including Warnings and Advice to the Married and Single*, went through forty printings. After this success Fowler's interests switched to architecture and, unencumbered by any knowledge of the subject, he produced a book called *A Home for all: or, the Gravel Wall, and Octagon Mode of Building*. Published in 1849, it declared an octagon to be the perfect plan for a house:

How much fretfulness and ill temper, as well as exhaustion and sickness, an unhandy house occasions. Nor does the evil end here. It often, generally, by perpetually irritating mothers, sours the temperament of their children, even before birth, thus rendering the whole family bad dispositioned by nature, whereas a convenient one would have rendered them constitutionally amiable and good.

Fowler built a four-storey octagonal house for himself in Fishkill, New York, but 'Fowler's Folly' proved so costly that he was forced to go on lecture tours to raise the money to pay for it. It may have been on one of these trips that the people of Bowmanville first became aware of octagonal houses. More likely it was his book that spread the word. In any event, in 1864 the trustees of the Congregational Church built an octagonal parsonage to serve as a home for their minister, Rev. Thomas Reike. The house is two storeys with stuccoed walls and a square central hall. On the roof there is a square lantern with chimneys on two opposite sides; windows on the other sides have been covered. When it was built, the house had louvred shutters which would have softened its somewhat stark appearance. The verandah is a later addition.

Across the street from the octagonal parsonage, at 49 Division Street, is Waltham Cottage, built by James McFeeters in 1856. McFeeters was mayor of Bowmanville in 1858, 1859, and 1861. At

Octagonal house, built as a parsonage, 48 Division Street

the end of one term he announced publicly that he would not stand for re-election, but then changed his mind. The *Canadian Statesman* remarked on 9 December 1858:

We are glad that Mr McFeeters has consented to stand; and at the same time take the liberty of telling him that, if he values the good name that he has earned, he must not change his mind on the same subject more than 6 times within as many weeks. Firmness of purpose is a great feature in the character of a public man.

In 1860, only four years after building it, McFeeters sold Waltham Cottage, possibly because of financial difficulties: an early resident of the town recalled in his memoirs that McFeeters lost a great deal of money following the completion of the Grand Trunk Railway. Dr George Low bought the house, but in turn sold it two years later to his nieces, Catherine and Julia Welch. The sisters operated a private school for girls there, teaching not only academic subjects but the manners expected of a Victorian gentlewoman. The verandah of Waltham Cottage, with its elaborate treillage, was built in the early part of this century to replace the original one which surrounded the house on three sides. The wooden storm door at the main entrance is unusual: it contains an arrangement of transom and lights that duplicates that on the inner door.

Across from Waltham Cottage, at 53 Division Street, is a two-storey brick house built in 1858 for John McClung. Like his neighbour McFeeters, McClung came from Ireland and was an active Conservative in politics. Both men ran for public office, and both also suffered business reverses, McClung in the '80s when his dry goods store went bankrupt.

Several years before its demise, the firm of McClung Brothers ran a wordy advertisement in the 23 June 1868 edition of the *Canadian Statesman*. Headed 'General Excitement in Bowmanville,' it offered at auction $50,000 worth of dry goods including everything from glassware to buffalo robes. The announcement concluded: 'Observe – there will be no bogus bidding, no reserve – no misrepresentation – no trash. Beware of those in the trade who say: "It is rubbish, old goods etc." Come and see for yourself. We have no rubbish to offer.'

When it was built, the McClung house was a one-storey structure with French doors leading onto an encirclng verandah – not unlike the McFeeters house across the street. The second floor was added and the verandah removed sometime during the 1870s, changing the entire character. This remains, however, a well-proportioned building; every detail of the addition relates perfectly with the design of the original.

David Fisher, as general manager of the Ontario Bank in Bowmanville, was one of the town's leading citizens. His elegant house at 37 Silver Street is now the home of the Bowmanville Museum – a happy arrangement for both the house and the museum's fine collection of period furniture and artifacts. When he began construction of Waverly Place in 1848, Fisher was still in his mid-twenties, working as collector of customs at the port of Darlington. It is not surprising therefore, that he built a small, four-room, one-storey house – undoubtedly all he could afford. In 1857 he began work with the bank and, four years later, was well enough established to add a second floor, with a belvedere as a finishing touch.

The John McClung house, 53 Division Street

For many years, the grounds surrounding the house added greatly to its charm. Fisher was an enthusiastic horticulturist and his gardens were a source of pride for the entire community. These gardens are to be restored by the local horticultural society.

Like the city of Hamilton, Bowmanville has a Dundurn built by a man named MacNab. But the Bowmanville building is not a castle, nor was its owner the illustrious Sir Allan Napier MacNab, prime minister of the United Canadas from 1854 to 1856. Instead, Bowmanville's Dundurn is a relatively small brick house that stands at 26 Concession Street. It was built in 1854 by Rev. Alexander MacNab, the rector of St John's Anglican Church.

In Scotland, Dundurn is the title of one of the chieftanships of Clan MacNab and means 'Fort on the Water' – a fitting appellation for the mansion in Hamilton. Its use for the Bowmanville house suggests that the rector had a sense of humour. Certainly he would have known of the larger Dundurn, for it had been built nineteen

Waverly Place, now the Bowmanville Museum, 37 Silver Street

years earlier and, as the largest Regency house in Upper Canada, received considerable public notice.

Alexander MacNab was born in 1811 and raised as a Methodist. For four years he served as principal of Victoria College in Cobourg. In 1848 he received his Doctorate of Divinity from the Methodist Church, but the next year he resigned after a period of dissension with his colleagues, and became an Anglican. After a year as curate of St Peter's in Cobourg, he served in Newcastle for a year or two, and then in 1853 moved to Bowmanville, where he lived until his death.

MacNab was an old friend of Sir John A. Macdonald. The two corresponded about educational matters during MacNab's days at Victoria College, and kept up an exchange of letters afterward. On 11 March 1891 Macdonald wrote to MacNab about the recent election, in which he had led the Conservatives to victory. He concluded: 'You and I will it is clear now both die British subjects.' Less than

Bowmanville's Dundurn, built by Rev. Alexander MacNab

three months later, the prime minister was dead. MacNab died in November of the same year.

The house that he built in Bowmanville is a storey-and-a-half affair, set in spacious grounds. Originally it had shutters on the windows and only a small, columned porch at the front door. The exterior wood trim was restrained and graceful. In later years, a verandah replaced the porch and a small port-cochère was added to the east side.

In 1867, MacNab sold Dundurn to another Scot, a local merchant named John Milne. Milne was an active Conservative who ran twice for Parliament and was defeated both times. He too was acquainted with Sir John A. Macdonald, who on at least one occasion visited Dundurn with his wife to attend a large garden party there. When she was introduced to one of the guests who was described as being the only Grit in attendance, Lady Macdonald is said to have replied, 'He couldn't be a Grit. He is far too good-looking.'

The Vanstone (originally Simpson) Mill, on Highway 2

Still another Scot to settle in Bowmanville was a young man named John Simpson, who arrived with his parents in 1825. He also had conservative leanings. During the Mackenzie Rebellion he enthusiastically supported the government in its attempts to suppress the rebels and, it was said, 'took an earnest part in showing many misguided men their error and leading them back to the path of duty and loyalty.' Two years before that, at the age of twenty-three, Simpson had become the sole manager of all the Bowman interests in the village – and there were many. Charles Bowman, a Montreal businessman, owned most of the land, the stores, and the mills, so it is not surprising that the town was later named after him.

The large frame mill that still stands where Highway 2 crosses Barber's Creek was one of the Bowman interests, but Simpson built it for him in 1850 and in later years Simpson's son ran it, and it was known locally as Simpson's Mill. In 1851, Simpson entered two barrels of flour in the London Exhibition in England and won first prize. The flour was presented to Queen Victoria's chaplain. In later years Simpson continued to be successful in business – he was a founder and president of the Ontario Bank – and in politics, and in 1867, the year of Confederation, he was named to the Senate.

Samuel Vanstone was an Englishman who arrived in Canada in 1842 and settled near Newcastle. Two years later, he married Elizabeth Elford. By 1852, the young couple had acquired enough capital to buy a mill at Tyrone, a village north of Bowmanville, and there they stayed for twenty-six years. Of their twelve children, five died before the age of four, and a sixth died in his twenty-third year. In 1878 Samuel moved to Bowmanville and rented the Simpson Mill. Eight years later, Samuel's son Jabez bought the property. It has remained in the family ever since, and is owned today by the great-grandson of Samuel and Elizabeth. The mill itself has scarcely changed since it was built. Repairs have been made, of course, and rollers replaced the original millstones in the late 1880s. The machinery is still run by water power, however, and electricity is used only to provide lighting.

15

Oshawa

In 1804 the schooner *Speedy* sank in Lake Ontario during a storm, carrying with it some of Upper Canada's leading citizens on their way to a trial at Presqu'ile Point. Among those who drowned was Robert Isaac Day Gray, the solicitor-general. Gray was a confirmed opponent of the slavery that was still legal in Canada, and in his will left instructions that his slaves were to be given their freedom. To some of them he left money and to others land. One of the slaves, a man named Simon, received two hundred acres in East Whitby Township – land which became the northwest part of what is now Oshawa. Gray also left 'all my wearing apparel to my servant Simon, and also my silver watch ... plus fifty pounds.' Another slave, Dorinda was left £1,200, to be invested on her behalf and the annual income given to her.

For a long time after Simon inherited his land – and subsequently sold it five years later – Oshawa remained a small and unremarkable village. Unlike other towns along the lake it did not have a good harbour, and at mid-century, when the railroad was built, the tracks ran more than a mile south of Oshawa's centre. One of the early residents remarked that he had never known a town that offered fewer natural inducements to industry.

The mettle of Oshawa's citizens was tested early in its history when cholera struck in the 1840s on the immigrant ships coming from Ireland. The people in the ports along the lake were faced with a terrifying problem. Dozens of dead or dying men and women were deposited on the wharfs by captains anxious to rid themselves of the disease. The townspeople were left to cope. In Port Oshawa two men did so heroically. They were the harbourmaster, James Wood, and his predecessor, George Mothersill. Both cared for the wretched newcomers abandoned there, but soon both of them too contracted the disease and died.

James Wood had almost completed a fine stone house, now part of Lakeview Park, Simcoe Street South, when he died in 1849. Shortly afterward, it was bought by Rev. Thomas Henry, minister of what became the Oshawa Christian Church. Henry, his wife, and twelve children lived there for nearly thirty years. It was he who added the frame second storey to provide additional bedrooms for his large family.

Henry's life was not uneventful. As a young man he had served in the militia during the War of 1812. Years later, he told of the escape of two prisoners he was escorting from York to Kingston. The party was lodged overnight at Smith's Mill in Port Hope and, although the

The Thomas Henry house, Lakeview Park

prisoners were in handcuffs and leg irons, they managed to hide under the water-wheel where the water was deep enough to cover them completely.

Following the war, Henry married and settled on a farm north of Port Oshawa, where he built a log house and later a frame house. His wife died in 1829, leaving him with four young sons to raise; but he married again the following year and had several more children. Records of the number of Henry children are conflicting. It is known there were daughters, but Henry's obituary mentioned only eight surviving sons and numerous grandchildren. Perhaps the daughters were unimportant – or perhaps, in that age of early female mortality, they did not outlive their father.

During the aftermath of the Mackenzie Rebellion, Henry and his family often sheltered fugitives. 'We suffered much on account of our liberal views and peace principles,' he later recalled. At the time, the Henrys were living about three miles north of the lake. There rebels would hide until arrangements were made to get them to the shore and a boat that would carry them to the American side. Once young John Henry, Thomas's son, assisted in the escape of a Dr Hunter. For three days, the doctor hid in a shanty by the lake while John pretended to work on his uncle's boat. In reality, with the help of the boat's mate, he was preparing a small compartment in which the doctor could hide. He succeeded so well that the stowaway's presence was not discovered, either by the boat's owner, John's uncle Jesse Trull, or by Jesse's brother John. The latter, as a captain of the militia, inspected the boat before it sailed. Jesse Trull was sympathetic to the rebels' cause, but his boat might have been confiscated had Dr Hunter been found.

Just to the east of Thomas Henry's house is a large three-storey yellow brick structure, the home for a while of John Robinson. Local records state that John was a Quaker, but not apparently a particularly devout one. Although he was a cobbler by trade, the house he built by the lake in 1846 served mainly as a meeting place for the many sailors from the nearby harbour. In 1850 he obtained a permit to distil spirituous liquors and a license to 'utter and sell WINE, BRANDY, RUM and other spirituous liquors by Retail in quantities of not less than one quart, to be drunk out of Robinson house.' John had come to Upper Canada in 1833, settled in Cobourg, moved to Oshawa after six years, and finally left his wife and ten children there to fend for themselves while he took off for Iowa. Mrs Robinson turned the house into an inn, for which it was well suited by size and location.

Robinson House is now a museum, administered by the Oshawa and District Historical Society. Although the building was in disrepair for many years, it has been well restored and is in excellent condition. Of particular interest is its gambrel roof which extends over the upper gallery, a relatively uncommon feature for the period.

Many of the large, impressive churches built in Ontario during the last half of the nineteenth century were the work of a Toronto architect, Henry Langley. His practice was widespread and non-sectarian in nature: in Oshawa alone he designed the Anglican church, the Baptist chapel, and the Wesleyan Methodist church. The latter building, at the corner of Simcoe and Bagot Streets, was built in 1867, the year after another Langley-designed church, All Saints Anglican in Whitby, was completed. The Methodist Congregation

Robinson House, once a tavern, now a museum

began in 1818 when a devoted itinerant preacher, Rev. William Jackson, gathered nine people together to form a prayer group. This was the nucleus of today's Simcoe Street United Church.

The Presbyterians in Oshawa were served for almost half a century by a stern and upright Scot, Rev. Robert H. Thornton. Like so many of his countrymen, Thornton placed a high value on education. 'I cannot but regard our Common and Grammar Schools as among the most valuable institutions which any civilized community can possess,' he stated, and he spent much of his life pursuing this goal. As well he travelled long distances over almost impassable roads to visit his parishioners: when he arrived in the 1830s he was the only Presbyterian minister between York and Port Hope. In recognition of this devoted service he was awarded a doctorate of divinity by Princeton University.

Thornton and his wife Margaret lived for thirty-eight years in a small frame house that stands today at 708–10 King Street West. It

Rev. Robert H. Thornton's home, 708–10 King Street West

was built near the corner of Thornton Road and King Street, but was later moved to its present location a short distance to the east. In it they raised a large family, and were noted for unfailing hospitality to travellers along the Kingston Road. Thornton devoted his life to the eradication of what he felt were the primary evils of the day: drunkenness, illiteracy, and immorality. He died in 1875 and is buried in Union Cemetery, a short distance from his home.

North of the Thornton house was a farm owned for many years by Edmund Cooper. He and his wife, Phoebe French, built their pleasant frame house shortly after they bought the land in 1842. The house, at 344 Thornton Road North, is now covered with stucco and the picket fence which once surrounded it has gone. The interior plan is unusual, for it appears that the fireplace was built in a centre hall only four or five feet wide. This would have made the circulation of heat something of a problem. Later renovations removed one wall of the hall so that the fireplace could heat the living room.

The Edmund Cooper house, 344 Thornton Road

Edmund Cooper came to Canada from New York State in 1818 when he was thirteen. His family lived close to the lake for many years but he moved north after his marriage. The forty-seven acre farm was purchased from Edward French, presumably a member of his wife's family.

As Oshawa grew and prospered, so did its close neighbour, Whitby. There was, however, very little social contact between the two towns. Oshawa was engrossed with problems of expansion and production while Whitby, as the county town, became the home of officials and professional people. Not surprisingly, a strong class feeling developed. One Whitby resident recalls today her grandmother's shock when asked if she knew a certain family in Oshawa. 'My dear,' she stated, 'we would never have known anyone who lived there.'

16

Whitby

At the turn of the eighteenth century, many of the choice lots in the lakeside concessions around Whitby were held by absentee owners. This was very different from the Kingston-Quinte area, where the front concession lots had been granted to Loyalists who cleared their new land as soon as possible in order to build homes and farm. Although lots were traded and sold amongst the Loyalists, the axe was swinging from 1784.

Crown land nearer York was not greatly affected by the Loyalist immigration, and although some families took up land for settlement at an early date much of the lakeside property remained forested for many years. Such names as Elizabeth Russell, sister of Peter Russell, the administrator of Upper Canada, are to be found on the Broken Front deeds. King's College owned several lots. William Willcocks, Sr, judge of the Home District Court, had land in Whitby Township, and in August 1795 he was advertising in the Schenectady *Mohawk Mercury* to sell his extensive holdings:

Upwards of 30,000 Acres of most excellent land on the north side of Lake Ontario, in the Township of Whitby, about 18 miles East of the new Town of York, now building for the seat of Government, 20 miles west of the Bay of Canty, and 30 north of Niagra – divided into 200 acre lots – will be disposed of on moderate terms by Wm. Willcocks Esq., who will give good Encouragement to the first 10 industrious settlers that close with him before the first day of November next; apply to him at Niagra or York or to the printers of the Mohawk Mercury at Schenectady.

N.B. This Township is nine miles front on Lake Ontario and twelve deep, it has three Good Harbours and several Capital Mill Sites.

In Pickering Township, closer to York, King's College held eighteen lots in the three front concessions. Sir David William Smith, surveyor-general of Upper Canada, held seven lots. Catherine McGill, wife of John McGill, a member of the Executive Council of Upper Canada, held eight lots. All were absentee owners. But as commerce in the natural ports along the lake began to provide wealth for local entrepreneurs who had settled and built up shipping and milling interests, the land behind the ports was gradually cleared.

One of the first businessmen in Port Whitby was Captain James Rowe, an Irishman who came to Upper Canada in 1824. In a partnership, he built and operated warehouses at the new piers and owned a company that built lake ships. For a time he was part owner in a toll road into the northern concessions. The establishment of a vigorous and prosperous community at Port Whitby was largely due to him and his partners. His white frame house at Victoria and Charles Streets is a beautifully preserved example of a successful merchant's home of the time. Certain details appear to date from the 1840s, but a mortgage was taken out in 1856 and it is uncertain whether this was for construction of the house or for extensions. The house retains many of its original architectural elements, including the six-panelled entrance door. Some of the windows still have early sash, muntins, and glass.

Two buildings in Whitby were built in the 1840s of limestone quarried at a distance of approximately 150 miles – near Kingston. The first is St John's Church, Port Whitby, and the second the Thomson house on Garden Street. The limestone came as ballast in vessels which travelled the lake.

St John's Church has stood at Victoria and Brock Streets since 1846, a simple dignified building in whose cemetery are buried many of Whitby's early residents. Anglicans in the Port Whitby area were served in the 1830s by itinerant missionaries, one of whom was Rev. Adam Elliot, later rector of St George's, Pickering. For many years before building the church, the congregation met in local homes. The land for the church was the gift of John Scadding, the father of Rev. Henry Scadding, rector for many years of Holy Trinity Church, Toronto, and one of that city's earliest historians. The first rector was Rev. John Pentland, an Irishman who had served in His Majesty's Horse Guard in France, Spain, and Italy before entering the ministry and emigrating to Canada. From Whitby, Pentland travelled to Oshawa and settlements north of the lake. He and his wife Frances raised seventeen children. His annual salary was £75.

A frequent visiting preacher at this time was Rev. Vincent Philip Mayerhoffer, a Hungarian who had served in the Austrian army against Napoleon, been captured, escaped, crossed the ocean, and settled in Pennsylvania. At one point he had been a Roman Catholic priest, but he left that church and became an Anglican missionary in Markham and Vaughan in the 1830s. Eventually he settled in Whitby and – completing his reversal of faith – became a Royal Arch Mason and Grand Chaplain of the Orange Lodge. He is buried in St John's cemetery.

In 1866 All Saints, Whitby, was built in what was becoming the faster growing part of town, at Dundas and Centre Streets, up from

Captain James Rowe's home, Victoria and Charles Streets

the port. The church and parish hall were designed by Henry Langley, who was responsible for several other churches in the area. The hall is a replica of an English country church. The spire was added in 1870 when the hall was being built.

The second Kingston limestone building is Mayfield, once the home of John and Jane Thomson, on Garden Street (lot 25, concession 2, Whitby). It is said that a bottle of Scotch whiskey was implanted somewhere deep in the walls when Mayfield was being built so that, according to an old tradition, 'there would always be a drink in the house.'

Thomson was born in Edinburgh and came to Canada in 1834 with his wife Jane Purves and their four small sons. According to a descendant, John and his eldest son walked east along the Kingston road from York looking for good land. They heard music and followed it to a church in which they found an old friend, Rev. Robert Thornton, conducting a service. On his advice Thomson decided to

St John's Church

settle in Whitby. He bought his property in two stages, in 1837 from James Somerville and in 1845 from William Kent. His first home was of logs. The second was a frame house at the south end of the land. The third was the stone building on the property today. In time, the four children increased to ten. They grew up with comforts Jane had brought across the ocean and from York – a grandfather clock, her piano and violin, her china and linens and art work. A Thomson descendant recalls Mayfield as a home which was always open to friends. The Presbyterian church socials were held there and the flash of kilts and swords was seen in the large hall. Mayfield remained in the family until 1905.

In July 1859, the Whitby *Chronicle* reported that the town could now boast a building which 'is not only the largest in Canada, but, we are well assured ... is unequalled in size and extent by any other detached family mansion on the continent of America.' When many of the early settlers along Lake Ontario were feeling pride in the

Mayfield, home of Jane and John Thomson, Garden Street

completion of a two-storey residence, Nelson Gilbert Reynolds was building a castle. Both 'Iron' Reynolds and his home were unique.

Reynolds was born in Kingston in 1814, the son of a bishop of the Methodist Episcopal Church, and named after Lord Nelson. His eventful life is told in a book published in 1880 with a title worthy of the subject, *The Canadian Biographical Dictionary and Portrait Gallery of Eminent and Self-Made Men*. According to this account, Reynolds was a remarkable young man. By the age of fifteen he was an officer in the 11th Lancers in England, having already been educated at Upper Canada College and a New York seminary. He returned briefly to Belleville, where his parents were living, then left for the west to serve the Hudson's Bay Company. Back in Belleville he was elected to the Legislative Assembly before he reached the age of twenty-one, and had to wait for his birthday before taking his seat. In his twenties he was president of the Marmora foundry and head of a steamboat company, along with other business interests.

During the 1837 rebellion, Reynolds remained loyal to the Crown but spoke out against the Family Compact, the Toronto-based group that pretty well ran Upper Canada. He was wounded at Kingston and called a traitor, and fled to the United States. Later he returned and surrendered. He stood trial for conspiracy and treason and was acquitted, although the general feeling was that he was guilty but proof was lacking. In 1854, he was appointed sheriff of Ontario County.

Nothing about Reynolds was less than extraordinary. He was a man of great physical stamina and athletic ability. To his success in the army, business, and politics he added the feat of fathering twenty-four children, twelve each with two different wives – he did nothing by halves.

His home was literally his castle and he named it Trafalgar after Nelson's famous victory. Construction began in 1859 and for the next few years it was the delight of newspapers in the area to relate the incredible details to their readers. The Whitby *Chronicle* noted that there were fifteen towers on the building; the largest was seventy-five feet high and covered in tin, while the others were topped in cut stone. There were seventy-three apartments. A central hall one hundred and five feet long led to a gothic carved oak staircase with four immense stained glass windows incorporating the arms of England, Scotland, Ireland, Canada, and the Reynolds and Armstrong (his second wife's) families. All the parlours and sitting rooms on the main floor were connected 'by sliding doors that they may be thrown open as occasion may require, into one grand suite of apartments, forming an unbroken area of 2,357 superficial feet.' There were five entrances. The building contained an armoury, rooms for governesses, and a gymnasium-billiard room; comfort was assured by a 'hot, cold and foul air flue, with valves and registers to regulate the temperature within.' In 1862 the Whitby *Press* noted with astonishment some of the building materials used: '2,500 feet of Ohio free-stone, 125,000 white bricks, 630,000 red bricks and 275,000 feet of lumber.' The castle was to be lit by gas manufactured in its own gas house and brought in by half a mile of pipes. Thirty-seven bells would summon servants.

The entire project was completed without a single accident or fight – a feat Reynolds attributed to his having forbidden the use of liquor to the seventy workmen on the job at one time. Editorial writers remarked: 'Contractors and others employing men should

Trafalgar Castle, built by Nelson Reynolds, now the Ontario Ladies College

take note of this important fact and avail themselves of the lesson which it conveys for future use.' The design by Joseph Sheard of Toronto received a final accolade in the Oshawa *Vindicator* in 1862: 'It is almost impossible for the visitor to keep the idea out of his mind that the castle through which he walks is located on Broadway and Fifth Avenue.'

Trafalgar Castle had its most prestigious hour when in 1869 Prince Arthur, third son of Queen Victoria, crossed the threshold with Frances Eliza Reynolds and ate his luncheon in her home.

The magnificent castle cost $60,000 to build, however, and much more to furnish and operate. It was rumoured that a secret passage had been constructed to which the owner could repair to avoid his creditors. By the 1870s it became impossible for Reynolds to maintain his home, and he was asked by some prominent citizens to consider selling it so that it could be used as an educational institute for young ladies. The building subsequently became the Ontario Ladies College.

In 1853, Ontario County separated from the United Counties of York, Ontario, and Peel. Whitby became the county seat and the town's stature attracted many new residents. Construction increased accordingly. One of the most important new structures was the Ontario County Court House, now the Centennial Building, at 416 Centre Street South. The architects were Frederic William Cumberland and W.G. Storm, who also designed University College and much of Osgoode Hall in Toronto. As with so many other civic buildings it was planned in the classical revival style, reflecting its importance. The central portion and wings of the present building date from 1854. A second floor was added in 1910. The court house was the most imposing building in town until Nelson Reynolds outdid the county's grand effort with his castle.

The contract for the construction of the court house and other county buildings was given to James Wallace, who had come to Whitby at the age of thirty-one and succeeded in a variety of ventures, including a newspaper, the Glasgow Soap Works, and the Canada Clock Company. His chief interest, however, was in the militia. He founded the volunteer Whitby Highland Rifle Company in 1856 and supplied its uniforms and equipment. After building his own substantial brick home on Centre Street South at Keith Street

Staircase, Ontario Ladies College

in 1855 he personally financed the construction of several smaller buildings that were to serve as officers' quarters and barracks. They are still standing nearby. Officers were housed in the finely designed brick house across the street from Wallace's home. The cottage to the south was for the commanding officer. When the Prince of Wales visited Whitby in 1860, Wallace and his men formed an honour guard that escorted the royal carriage from the railway station to a boat waiting at the lake.

In 1857, Wallace built what must be one of the most attractive buildings ever to be used as a barracks. It stands at 219 Keith Street. After ten years in military service, it was sold to Robert Wilson, a lawyer and nephew of Judge Zaccheus Burnham. When his wife died in 1868 Wilson left, grief-stricken, unable to continue his work or his life in Whitby. On 29 February 1876, he died – eight years to the day after the death of his wife. He was only forty-two.

Another example of Whitby's affluence in the 1850s and '60s is

Ontario County Court House, now the Centennial Building

the house at Raglan and Giffard Streets built for William Laing, who made his money in grain shipping. The deep mellow colour of the brick in the two-storey building sets off the beauty of many small-paned windows. A large, well-treed lot provides a magnificent setting. In 1870 the house was sold to George McGillivray and his wife Caroline Fothergill, daughter of Port Hope's first postmaster. It was she who named it Inverlynn – from the Gaelic 'Inver,' meaning 'the mouth of,' and 'Lynn' from the Lynde Creek adjacent to the property. The McGillivrays may have moved in just in time to have front row seats for the running of the Queen's Plate, which took place that year on the track behind the home of their neighbours, the Lyndes.

McGillivray had emigrated from St Fergus, Aberdeenshire, in 1833. When he arrived in Whitby, he stayed for a while with another Scot, William Dow, to whom he had an introduction. Once established, he sent for his parents, brothers, and sisters. Scotland, how-

Inverlynn, the McGillivray home, Raglan and Giffard Streets

ever, was never forgotten. McGillivray became bard of the local St Andrew's Society, and was noted for his anniversary odes; one of the most famous was 'Mither's Auld Crook.'

Inverlynn has remained in the family. It was known for the warmth of the family's 'ain fireside' and hospitality. For many years, vagabonds on the Danforth could depend upon finding food and shelter there: the only stipulation that McGillivray made to his 'regulars' was that, should they arrive on a Saturday, they must stay until Monday in order not to disturb the sabbath with comings and goings. In the 1970s Inverlynn received renewed attention when it was chosen as the site for exterior filming of the 'Whiteoaks of Jalna' television series.

McGillivray's fellow Scot, William Dow, was a highly successful farmer. His house, Glen Dhu, on Rossland Road east of Garden Street, was completed in 1850, just five years before his death. In his will, Dow left to his 'dear wife Jane' all his 'furniture, bedding and carpeting except an eight day clock' and 'if she chooses to remain in the house she is to have the use of one room and two bedrooms and a cow kept also all necessaries whatsoever except wearing apperal and groceries.' The latter needs were to be met from a yearly annuity of £20, paid in two equal instalments to make it last.

Greenwood House, 210 Henry Street, is the frame building (now somewhat altered) that housed the family of John Hamar Greenwood. It was built in the 1850s. Greenwood was a native of Wales who came to Canada without education, money, or prospects. According to the Oshawa *Vindicator*, 'He is said to have mixed mortar and carried the hod while assisting in building the Court House' and was later noted as a financier who could 'always wiggle out of a hole but his enterprising and speculative nature pulled him back into the hole as fast as he could struggle his way out.' His son, Thomas Hamar Greenwood, returned to Great Britain, became a lawyer, acted as Winston Churchill's parliamentary secretary for four years, was made baronet in 1915, served in Lloyd George's cabinet, and became a viscount in 1937.

The row housing on Byron Street North, known as The Terrace, was also built in the 1850s, by Robert Perry, son of Whitby's founder Peter Perry. In the mid-nineteenth century it housed the offices of some of the town's most distinguished doctors and lawyers. It has deteriorated since.

Partially concealed behind shrubbery is the home of Zaccheus Burnham at 210 Byron Street North. The judge was the son of John Burnham, one of the four brothers who settled at an early date in the Cobourg-Port Hope area. Zaccheus completed his legal studies under Hon. Robert Baldwin, practised in Port Hope, and moved to Whitby in 1843. For forty-two years, from 1854 until his death, he was judge of Ontario County. In 1865, during this period of financial success, he constructed his fine brick home, which remains in excellent condition today.

Burnham was known as a quiet man who was dedicated to the Plymouth Brethren, with whom he spent all his spare time. His obituary seems to imply that his success was due more to hard work than to genius. 'He never aimed at brilliancy, but in both professional and judicial work he displayed a conscientiousness ... which begat full respect and confidence. If his judgement ever led him into error it was not the result of friendship or sympathy.'

Roderick Ross house, 407 Colborne Street West

In the mid-nineteenth century many men proved that it was possible to come to this new country, with nothing except a desire to work and some common or business sense, and achieve a comfortable life style. In 1858 Roderick Ross arrived in Whitby from Ross Shire, Scotland, with his wife, Jean, and two sons, Hugh and George. Roderick, then forty-three years old, took work right away on the construction of St Andrew's Church at Byron and John Streets. After a year, his father wrote urging him to return to Scotland because he saw bad times coming. But in Whitby Roderick saw a promising future. He opened a dry goods business. That it prospered is evident in the home he was able to built at 407 Colborne Street West not long after his arrival. A porch has been removed and a small bay window added, but the beauty of the deep red bricks still sets off a hospitable door and graceful windows. Two more children, Andrew and Margaret, were born in Whitby. The two elder boys joined their

Jabez Lynde house, Dundas at D'Hillier Streets, now the Whitby Museum

father in business, while Andrew eventually opened his own store nearby. The house to the east of his parents' was built for George; Hugh carried on in the main house; Andrew lived around the corner in a Victorian delight quite different from his parents' traditional residence.

The oldest house in Whitby – on the Danforth Road, Dundas at D'Hillier Street – was the home of Jabez Lynde, a Quaker who came from Brookfield, New York, in 1803. His first house was built of logs. In 1812, when war with the United States appeared imminent, it was visited by Sir Isaac Brock, the British commander, on his way west to supervise preparations for defence. Lynde's daughter Clarissa was then seven years old. As an old woman she recalled that Brock and his aide-de-camp 'were clad in long plaid coats lined with fur. The suavity of the commander-in-chief was manifest even in the wayside log inn, and won the heart of the little Canadian girl of the house, who for four score years has not ceased to sorrow for his untimely end.' Lynde himself was pressed into service as a messenger and rode through the snow to Government House at York in three hours and five minutes.

During the war Jabez was engaged to furnish supplies, for which the British paid freely. He became wealthy. According to Clarissa's account, a certain room in the house would 'often be filled with kegs of money,' and a portion of the log barn was set aside for storing crates of biscuits and other provisions. Soldiers were billeted in the house and, Clarissa reported, 'In the night one of these guests arose and, with a dexterous hand, cut from the neck of Mrs Lynde while she slept a valuable string of gold beads.'

With his profit from the war Jabez built the house which stands today at the side of Lynde's Creek. It is now the Whitby Museum. The construction date was probably 1815. By that time Lynde had eight children. The front porch was more elaborate than at present, with four columns and a gable, and the interior trim was varied and intricate. Located by the side of each fireplace were panelled doors enclosing cupboards. Many original interior details may still be seen. The dining room walls still bear the remains of the stencilled, painted patterns which economically produced the effect of wallpaper – a form of decoration that rarely has survived. The house had a widow's walk on the roof. The rough cast was added in 1939.

17

Pickering

When William Wright's bride arrived from England to join him on his farm near Pickering (originally called Duffin's Creek), she was so dismayed with the house he had built for her that she refused to unpack her trunks. Or so the story goes. Wright purchased the property (lot 10, concession 1, Pickering) in 1826 and, although no one knows for sure, it appears that his wife did finally decide to stay with him. Fifty years later the farm was owned by a J. Wright who – barring coincidence – was probably their son.

While little is known of the Wright family, we can be certain that the handsome two-storey house standing on a rise overlooking the Kingston Road is quite unlike the house William built for his young wife. The original dwelling was a simple stone house of one storey, designed as a Regency cottage with French doors leading onto a surrounding verandah. Not until the turn of the century was the second storey added. The work was so well done that only an expert eye can tell the old from the 'new.' Simple, yet imposing, it became a house that even Mrs Wright should have been proud to own.

Not far north of the Wright farm (on lot 10, concession 2, Pickering) is a small stone house that has remained in the same family since it was built in 1845. Its original owners, Robert and Rachel Betts, were among the many Quakers in Pickering and in this house they raised their family of seven children. Three of the Betts daughters became school teachers, and one of them, Adelia, educated all four of *her* children to follow the same profession. The Betts had one son, John, who died as a young man; when that happened, Adelia's husband, Stephen Cronk, sold his own farm in Prince Edward County and bought the Betts farm in order to help his father-in-law. In later years, Stephen and Adelia's son, Robert, joined in the work. Today the great-great-granddaughter of Robert and Rachel owns and lives in the house built so well by her ancestors.

Incredible difficulties were encountered by another Quaker family, who arrived in Upper Canada from Connecticut in 1800. Timothy Rogers, with his wife and fourteen children, first settled near Newmarket when that area was still wilderness. After seven years he moved most of his family to Pickering, and there founded another Quaker settlement. The simple brick building near the corner of Highway 2 and Mill Street was a meeting house for the Friends, built in 1867 on land given for the purpose by the Rogers family. It is now used as a Masonic Temple.

Only devout faith sustained the Rogers family during the trials and tragedies they encountered in their new country. In his journal,

William Wright house, lot 10, concession 1, Pickering

Timothy Rogers told a story of initial hope in the new mill at Pickering:

In 1807 I bot a mil plase in Picorin ... This town Picorn lays on about the sentor of Lake Ontarao wheir emtys a fine streme cold Dofins Crik. This is a fine streme and I bilt my mil, so a bote cold com 3 mils from the Lake Shore and land at my mil dor, a fine fishery it is.

Two or three years later, he attended a yearly meeting of the Friends near West Lake, Prince Edward County. On his return, he found that seven of his children – most of them married, with families of their own – were dead, victims of typhus. Two years later, while they were on a trip to York, Timothy's wife Sarah took ill. Rogers recalled:

While I was lay down a short time, but I heird Salla say Mrs Rogers is

Home of Robert and Rachel Betts, lot 10, concession 2, Pickering

dying I arose and made hast but befor I got to hur she was departed this life. And I sent to my setold childorn at the fardor end of Yong Stret. They came to hur burel that was on the 17 day of the firs month at my one house in Picorn with my three childorn, Sarah, John and John Elmsley Rogers. And now I was left to move in my new hous with four childorn, two oldest sons setold at Yong Stret and Timothy disoned and gon to the stats. Do you think tong can tell my trobel or pen right my greaf.

Timothy Rogers later remarried and his new wife, Anna Harned, bore five more children. One of these was Jonathan Rogers. For many years he owned the land to the west of the Quaker Meeting House and it may have been he who built the modest frame house at 95 Kingston Road (Highway 2). Jonathan's half-brother, Wing Rogers, recalled that 'In 1828 we mooved up to the Kingston and Toronto Road, & there I took a school, & there we lived for about four years on a little place, near to where the yearly meeting is now

The old Quaker Meeting House

granted to the society of friends.' It is likely that the house was built by one of the half-brothers, for it appears to pre-date 1845, the year in which the property was sold by Jonathan to Daniel McDermid. Ten years later another Quaker, Gervas Cornell, bought the house and built additions.

Although the Quakers were the first and, for many years, the largest religious denomination in the area, the other churches were not without adherents. The earliest church services were organized by the pioneers themselves, but within a few years ministers arrived on the scene. Among them was Rev. Adam Elliot, a devout and intrepid Anglican from Cumberland County in England, who had been ordained in 1832 and shortly afterwards founded the parish of St George's, Pickering. For the following five years he travelled throughout what was called the Home District, from York to Port Hope and north as far as Penetanguishene – no easy feat when the weather was frigid and the trails nearly non-existent. During that

Rogers house, 95 Kingston Road

period Elliot began work with the Indians, first on Manitoulin Island and three years later with the Six Nations. (A niece was Pauline Johnson, the poetess.) Elliot died in 1878, aged seventy-six. He is buried in the cemetery of Holy Trinity Church at Onondaga, near Brantford. The parish he founded in Pickering at the beginning of his career is still active. Its fine brick church, built in 1841, stands at the southwest corner of Highway 2 and Randall Drive.

George Washington Post settled in Pickering Township early in the last century. Some sources suggest that he was of Loyalist stock, but this seems unlikely considering his given names – they would have been a curious choice for Loyalist parents during the American Revolution. His father and mother, Jordan and Abigail Post, were from Hebron, Connecticut, and they, with their six children, came to the town of York at an early date, possibly in the 1790s. George moved to Pickering where, in 1815, he built an imposing brick house on the Kingston Road. For many years it served as

Post Manor, Highway 2 and Brock Road

an inn and later became a stopping place for Weller's coaches on their way between Kingston and York.

The Posts had five sons and two daughters. Their youngest son, a handsome young man named Jordan, worked at the inn with his family. A few years after his father's death in 1837, Jordan and his bride Matilda built a fieldstone house about four miles west of the inn. 'My parents were ambitious to engage in a different life from selling spirituous liquors,' their son Charles later recalled, 'so gave up the job, "went west" and started the saw mill, with farming on the side.' Jordan's new business must have prospered from the start, for his house, Post Manor, was both spacious and elegant. Outside, heavy cornices and gables complement the fieldstone. The interior detailing is exceptionally fine. From the centre hall, a graceful staircase with a black walnut banister curves up to the second floor. Post Manor has lost none of its original beauty, thanks to an appreciative succession of owners.

This fine house stands, almost hidden by tall fir trees, at the northwest corner of Highway 2 and Brock Road. When it was built, Jordan's wife Matilda was only twenty-one years old and Jordan himself was twenty-seven. He died twenty years later, leaving a family of eight children, the youngest just a year old. Matilda lived on in the house until her death in 1886. In the small cemetery across the road, the graves of Jordan and Matilda Post are marked by a marble obelisk.

18

Along the 401

The Macdonald-Cartier Freeway (Highway 401) cut through existing farmland when it was constructed, and many early buildings were lost. A few, however, remain. They provide, to fast-moving travellers, a brief reminder of less hurried days. The following houses are included in the interests of those who are forced to drive along Highway 401, and who may have wondered about the occasional old building at the side of the road.

To the east of Cobourg, on the north side of the highway and east of Interchange 83, is the home of Anthony Blizzard. He was a farmer who settled in Hamilton Township early in the last century and lived there until his death in 1876. Little is known of him or his family other than a few odd facts found in assessment rolls. Blizzard apparently was living in the township by 1821 and was, at that time, the owner of one horse. Four years later he had purchased land (lot 5, concession 1, Hamilton) and had acquired 'two oxen, four cows and one young cattle.' By 1827, he had added to his responsibilities a wife, one son, and one daughter. He continued to prosper, buying more property in lot 6 in 1851 and there, seven years later, building the imposing stone house by the highway. It is a two-storey building with a kitchen 'tail' extending to the rear. Especially pleasing are the warm colours of the stone.

Many miles to the west (just east of Interchange 77), a handsome white frame house overlooks the highway near Newcastle. For more than half a century this was the home of James Patrickson Lovekin and his wife, Isabella Shaw.

The original Lovekin homestead was down near the lake, where James's father and grandfather had first settled in the 1790s. Isabella refused to live there: she no doubt feared a recurrence of the malaria that had afflicted Newcastle particularly severely in 1843–4. The James Lovekins therefore built their house well back from the lake. It stands on the north side of Highway 401 (on lot 35, concession 1, Clarke). The land has been in the family since the original grant in 1801 – a record few other Ontario families claim.

About a mile to the west of the Lovekin home, on lot 2, Broken Front concession, Darlington Township, also on the north side of the highway, is Drummore, a stone house built by John Archibald Galbraith in 1866. His grandmother, Margaret McGill Galbraith, had come to Canada from Scotland in 1834, bringing her five sons and a daughter. Soon the sons built new homes with colourful names: Duntroon, Poltollock, Yarnikal, and Floradale. John named his house after his grandmother's home in Argyllshire.

Drummore, west of Interchange 77

Drummore was built for John's bride, Christina Stalker. Inside, the family's Scottish heritage is evident: a newel post is carved in the shape of an upright lion, with thistles incorporated in the design. Changes made to the house have retained the original style. The large window on the south side, for example, is a later addition, but the panes in it were kept small and the wood trim used came from an old house in the area.

West of Interchange 73 are two Trull houses. In the early years of the nineteenth century, Lydia Casey Trull was sometimes seen on the back of her fine black saddle mare – swimming along the shore of Lake Ontario. At a time when there were no doctors in the area, it was Lydia who served as midwife and herbalist for settlers who fell ill. In order to reach their isolated farms, she was often forced to cross swollen streams and swamps. Hence the swimming lessons for a horse.

Lydia's husband, John W. Trull, had been born on the Isle of

Anthony Blizzard house, east of Interchange 83

Wight, served as a youngster in the navy and on a slave ship, made his way to the American colonies, and there served with the British during the Revolutionary War. In 1794 he set out with his family for Upper Canada. They spent weeks in an open boat going from the Susquehanna River to Lake Ontario where they coasted around the head of the lake, turning into bays and inlets to avoid storms and to camp at night. They arrived in Port Darlington, south of present-day Bowmanville, in October, and hastily constructed a small log shanty with a bark roof, plastered on the inside with mud. The Trulls survived that first winter, and many more. John died in 1830 at the age of eighty-four, Lydia six years later.

The better of the two Trull houses is the pleasant red brick farmhouse (lot 29, Broken Front concession, Darlington) on the south side of the highway. Records show that the property was purchased in 1857 by Henry Trull, a grandson of John and Lydia. The farm has been owned since then by various members of the family.

Henry Trull's house, west of Interchange 73

The other Trull house is just to the west, on the north side of Highway 401 (lot 31, concession 1, Darlington). It was the home of Jesse Trull, another grandson of the doughty lady who rode through the wilderness bringing comfort and courage to the pioneers along the lake. It is an exuberant structure of patterned brick, designed with less restraint than its neighbour. Any architectural merit it originally possessed, however, is hidden by the hundreds of derelict automobiles that now surround it. A sad end for a once impressive and unusual building.

It rather occurs to me that it's the commonplace people who DO things.
STEPHEN LEACOCK

SELECTED BIBLIOGRAPHY

Adamson, Anthony and Marion MacRae. *The Ancestral Roof*. Toronto, 1963
– *Hallowed Walls*. Toronto, 1975
Angus, Margaret. *The Old Stones of Kingston*. Toronto, 1966
Berton, Pierre. *The National Dream*. Toronto, 1970
Blake, Verschoyle Benson and Ralph Greenhill. *Rural Ontario*. Toronto, 1969
Boyce, Gerald E. *Historic Hastings*. Belleville, 1967
– *Hutton of Hastings*. Belleville, 1972
Burleigh, H.C. *Forgotten Leaves of Local History*. Kingston, 1973
Burley, Agnes. *Clarke Township Eastern Section: Its Places, People and Events*. Newtonville, 1967
Burr, W.K. *Historical Sketches of Prince Edward County*. Picton, 1971
The Canadian Biographical Dictionary and Portrait Gallery of Eminent and Self-Made Men, Ontario volume. Toronto, 1880
Canniff, William. *The Medical Profession in Upper Canada*. Toronto, 1894
– *A History of the Early Settlement of Upper Canada*. Toronto, 1869
Capon, Alan R. *Stories of Prince Edward County*. Belleville, 1973
Chadwick, Edward Marion. *Ontarian Families*. Toronto, 1894–8
Coleman, J.T. *History of the Early Settlement of Bowmanville and Vicinity*. Bowmanville, 1875
Craick, William Arnot. *Little Tales of Old Port Hope*. Port Hope, 1966
– *Port Hope Historical Sketches*. Port Hope, 1901; reprinted 1974
Craig, Gerald M. *Upper Canada: The Formative Years*. Toronto, 1963

Creighton, Donald G. *John A. Macdonald: The Young Politician.*
Toronto, 1952

Denison, Merrill. *The Barley and the Stream.* Toronto, 1955

Dictionary of Canadian Biography. Toronto, 1966 –

Dorland, Arthur Garratt. *Former Days and Quaker Ways.* Picton, 1965

Fairbairn, J.B. *History and Reminiscences of Bowmanville.*
Bowmanville, 1906

Fryer, Mary Beacock. *Loyalist Spy.* Brockville, 1974

Glazebrook, G.P. deT. *Life in Ontario: A Social History.* Toronto, 1968

Greenhill, Ralph, Ken Macpherson and Douglas Richardson. *Ontario
Towns.* Ottawa, 1974

Guillet, Edwin C. *Cobourg.* Oshawa, 1948

– *Pioneer Inns and Taverns.* Toronto, 1954–62

– *The Story of Canadian Roads.* Toronto, 1966

– *Toronto: From Trading Post to Great City.* Toronto, 1934

Haight, Canniff. *Life in Canada Fifty Years Ago.* Toronto, 1885

Hamlyn, R.G., E. Lunney and D.R. Morrison. *Bowmanville: A Retro-
spect.* Bowmanville, 1958

Herrington, Walter S. *History of the County of Lennox and Addington.*
Toronto, 1913

Hoig, D.S. *Reminiscences and Recollections.* Oshawa, 1933

Innis, Mary Quayle. *The Clear Spirit: Twenty Canadian Women and
Their Times.* Toronto, 1966

Jarrett, Thomas. *The Evolution of Trenton.* Trenton, 1913

Johnson, J.K. *Historical Essays on Upper Canada.* Toronto, 1975

Kaiser, T.E. *Historic Sketches of Oshawa.* Oshawa, 1921

Lunn, Richard and Janet. *The County.* Picton, 1967

McKay, William Angus. *The Pickering Story.* Brougham, 1961

Mika, Nick and Helma (editors). *Belleville: Friendly City.* Belleville,
1973

– *Community Spotlight.* Belleville, 1974

– *Pioneer Life on the Bay of Quinte.* Toronto, 1904; reprinted Belleville,
1972

Mikel, W.C. *City of Belleville History.* Picton, 1943

Minhinnick, Jeanne. *At Home in Upper Canada.* Toronto, 1970

Moodie, Susanna. *Life in the Clearings.* London, 1853; reprinted
Toronto, 1959

– *Roughing It in the Bush.* London, 1852; reprinted Toronto, 1962

Morris, Audrey. *The Gentle Pioneers.* Toronto, 1968; reprinted Toronto,
1973

Muntz, Madeleine. 'William Weller, Stagecoach Magnate' in *Victorian Cobourg* edited by J. Petryshyn. Belleville, 1976

Playter, George. *The History of Methodism in Canada*. Toronto, 1862

Preston, Richard Arthur. *Kingston Before the War of 1812*. Toronto, 1959

Queen's University School of Urban and Regional Planning. *History and Architecture of the Village of Bath, Ontario*. Kingston, 1976

Reeve, Harold. *The History of the Township of Hope*. Cobourg, 1967

Reid, William D. The Loyalists in Ontario. Lambertville, NJ, 1973

Rempel, John I. *Building with Wood*. Toronto, 1967

Roy, James A. *Kingston: The King's Town*. Toronto, 1952

Scadding, Henry. *Toronto of Old*. Toronto, 1875; reprinted Toronto, 1966

Squair, John. *The Townships of Darlington and Clarke*. Toronto, 1927

Stanley, George F.G. 'The Macpherson-Shaw-Macdonald Connection in Kingston' in *Historic Kingston: Transactions of the Kingston Historical Society*. Kingston, 1965

Stewart, J. Douglas and Ian E. Wilson. *Heritage Kingston*. Kingston, 1973

Traill, Catharine Parr. *The Backwoods of Canada*. London, 1836; reprinted Toronto, 1971

Turner, Larry. *Lake of the Mountain and Glenora*. (Unpublished report for the Ontario Ministry of Natural Resources) Toronto, 1974

Upton, L.F.S. *The United Empire Loyalists: Men and Myths*. Toronto, 1967

Wallace, W. Stewart. *The Macmillan Dictionary of Canadian Biography*. Toronto, 1963

GENERAL REFERENCE SOURCES

County Historical Atlases. Toronto 1878; reprinted Belleville 1977

Lennox and Addington Historical Society Papers

Ontario Historical Society Papers and Records

Resources of the Provincial Archives of Ontario, including the architectural inventory supervised by William S. Goulding

PAMPHLETS AND NEWSPAPER ARTICLES

Belleville's Heritage. The Hastings County Historical Society. Belleville, 1978

Centennial of the Incorporation of the Village of Brighton 1859–1959. Brighton, 1959

Cane, Fred. 'Historic Buildings.' *The Canadian Statesman.* Bowmanville, 1977

Centennial of Newcastle 1856–1956. Newcastle, 1956

Farr, Marion Richard. *From Saddlebags to Seventy-Five; A History of Newcastle United Church 1824–1975.* Newcastle, 1975

Kelly, Orval E. *In the Beginning* (Presqu'ile and Brighton). Presqu'ile, 1942

Luedtke, Walter. 'Looking Backwards.' *Colborne Chronicle* and *Cobourg Star.* Cobourg, 1974

Millman, T.R. 'Grafton Historical Notes.' *The Cobourg World*, 1934–5

Peebles, Delbert. *Village of Colborne 1859–1959.* Colborne, 1959

Historic Prince Edward. Prince Edward Historical Society. Picton, 1976

Taylor, David and Patricia. *The Hart Pottery Canada West.* Picton, 1966

Williamson, Lenny. 'Our Architectural Heritage.' *Ontario Intelligencer.* Belleville, 1964

Winters, Brian. 'Historical Whitby.' *Free Press*, Whitby, 1976

ACKNOWLEDGEMENTS

One of the great delights of conducting the research required for this book was the opportunity we had to meet many fascinating and knowledgeable people, the owners of the buildings. Without exception they went out of their way to be hospitable and helpful. An added bonus was the privilege of seeing the interiors of so many beautiful early homes. Space prohibits us from naming every person we met, but we want to express our sincere thanks to them all. Without their help our task would have been much more difficult.

In every community we visited there were, as well, a few very special people, some of whom are professional historians, but all of whom are vitally interested in their local history. Their assistance, often amounting to many hours of their time, was invaluable.

Along the Bath Road, we received both historical and genealogical help from Gwen Smith of the UEL Association. In the village of Bath, Mary Davy and George Davy supplied us with family and church records, as descendants of a founding family. W.J. Patterson, superintendent of historic sites for the St Lawrence Parks Commission, was extremely helpful with his insights into the history of the Fairfield White House in Amherstview and Fairfield Place in Bath. At the latter house, Janet Bowen was helpful and hospitable.

Help on the complex subject of Loyalist history was given by Dr J. Allan Walters, who has made a life-long study of the subject. His encouraging comments and suggestions were very welcome.

Anne MacDermaid of the Douglas Library, Queen's University, gave professional assistance in several aspects of our research. Peggy Clarke, a descendant of the Loyalist Wartman family, travelled from Montreal to Kingston in order to provide us with unique family documents.

Our introduction to the many splendid buildings in Picton was supplied by Roy Shortt of the Prince Edward County Historical Society, and Donald McDermaid, director of the Prince Edward County Museum. They were generous with both their time and their knowledge of local historical lore. Picton is also the home of Jeanne Minhinnick, author of *At Home in Upper Canada*. Our visit with her was pleasant and rewarding. Dr Arthur G. Dorland, born in The County and an expert on the Quakers in Canada, conferred with us about the Quaker Meeting House on the Marsh Front.

During our many trips to Prince Edward County, our work was helped inestimably by the enthusiasm and hospitality of His Honour Judge John D. O'Flynn, county court judge of Prince Edward County, and his wife Mary. We wish to thank them both for many kindnesses. At Glenora we were helped in our research by Larry Turner, a student at Queen's University. His well documented and exhaustively researched study of the Glenora Mills proved extremely useful.

The searching of land titles is a complex affair, rife with opportunity for error. We are therefore grateful to John V. Graydon and the staff of the registry office in Picton for their patience and unstinting help. In Wellington, research on the magnificent Tara Hall is being done by university students working during their summers. As a result, the obscure history of this house is finally coming to light. Our thanks to Sally Nash for sharing with us the results of her diligence.

Mrs Lorne Patterson, great-great-great-granddaughter of Samuel Way, whose house stands on the Marsh Front, made the results of her genealogical research on the Way family available to us. Her daughter, Susan A.C. Patterson, provided an architectural study of the house.

A resident of Odessa, Joyce Johnston, supplied us with a generous amount of the historical data that she has acquired over the years in the hope that the young people of her village will develop a pride in its colourful past. Mr and Mrs Roy Hartman, long-time residents of the Odessa area, also gave us insights into its history.

Napanee is fortunate in having an enthusiastic and active historical society, its efforts reflected in the many fine buildings that enhance the community. We owe thanks to Judge G.F. Smith for his help and to Helen Hutchison and Jane Foster, past and present curators respectively of the Lennox and Addington County Museum. They and Cora Reid, genealogist in the library, ably assisted us with our work there. A special debt of gratitude is owed to Alice Poole, title searcher par excellence, who never tired of helping us when we got beyond our depth. We remember with gratitude the boat trip that Alice and her husband, Werk Poole, took us on so that we might see the beautiful Bay of Quinte as the Loyalists first viewed it – from the water. Our research of the superb Macpherson house in Napanee was aided by the co-operation of Jean Macpherson, who graciously allowed us access to her extensive family records.

We were fortunate, when beginning our work in Belleville, to find that the Hastings County Historical Society had recently completed a survey of that city's early buildings. Elaine Preston and Lois Foster, two of the members responsible, were more than helpful in supporting our efforts there. As well, Gerald Boyce, historian and author, gave generously of his time and supplied valuable and constructive criticism. Again, at the registry office, Jim Wibberly offered cheerful assistance while we waded through local records.

In Trenton, much of the material used to study the history of the town was obtained with the help of Mary Salisbury and Ruth Little of the Trenton Memorial Public Library. Further west, in Brighton, Georgina Graham directed us to the village's best early buildings, from her experience as a volunteer with the Ontario Historic Buildings Inventory. Colborne's resident historical expert, Delbert Peebles, kindly met with us to discuss its intriguing past, as did Walter Luedtke. Mr. Luedtke's newspaper articles, 'Looking Backwards,' provided valuable details. Information regarding the Steele house in Colborne was provided by Professor James P. Lovekin of Lakehead University.

Dr T.R. Millman, who served as rector of Grafton's St George's Anglican Church for many years, is also an historian of note. His work was of great value, as was his advice on that chapter. Most of our material about the Webster family of Grafton was provided by Terry Boyle, curator of the McLaughlin Museum in Oshawa. Incidental bits of local lore were given to us by Maggie Prentice, 'Maggie-at-the-post-office' as she is affectionately known. At Barnum House, Carolyn Taylor obligingly talked with us and showed us through one of the finest neo-classic buildings in the province.

Much of what we learned in Grafton was due to the efforts and encouragement of Peggy Farr, who not only completed some unfinished chores for us but also served us lunches and on one occassion cheerfully discussed history at breakfast. Her enthusiasm for our work was very supportive.

Rob Mikel of Cobourg, a student of architecture, has compiled a wealth of historical material relating to that town and its buildings. His assistance was invaluable. We are grateful, as well, to Lenah Fisher, the guiding force behind the restoration of Victoria Hall, and to Foster Russell, a former editor of the Cobourg *Daily Star*. Mr Russell allowed us to peruse his early issues of that paper, beginning with the first edition in 1831. We also extend our thanks to Miss M. Rooney of Cobourg and to Mrs E.S. Turpin who gave us background information about the Boulton house on Henry Street.

Port Hope is blessed with a multitude of fine early buildings which its citizens watch with an eagle eye. They are actively involved in preserving their unique heritage. Among the many who knowledgeably and willingly assisted us were Tom Long, F. Austin Chestnut, and Alice King Sculthorpe. Others who contributed to this chapter were Walter K. Molson, Jane McColl (who allowed us to use historical notes made by her father, Harold Reeve), and Mrs Edgar Barrowclough.

In Newcastle, His Honour Judge Richard Lovekin gave generously of his time to discuss the Lovekin family and the history of Newcastle.

Bowmanville has an active group who are busily studying local history as it relates to the fine early buildings. Mrs E. Derry Hubbard discussed the work of the many interested citizens who have done a superb job of compiling data. Marion Veinot, curator of the Bowmanville Museum, showed us their extensive and growing collection housed in the old Fisher house and discussed that family. The Bowmanville library has its own historical files and Jan Leak, branch head, guided us there. The results of the research conducted by Frederick Cain mean greater security for the town's early buildings. We were grateful to be allowed to familiarize ourselves with his conclusions, and with the work of Molly Nind of the Heritage Committee.

It was a great pleasure to meet Thomas Bouckley of Oshawa, a man of many interests. His collection of photographs of buildings in Oshawa is unique and a treasure for that city. We appreciated the time given to us by the curators of two of Oshawa's historic houses, Frances Cornelius of the Robinson House and Maureen Mathew of Henry House.

As we approached research in Whitby we continually heard the name of Brian Winter, archivist of that town. When we met Brian we found his collection of early records extensive. Bruce Hunt, planner for the Town of Whitby, discussed the amazing work which has been done by local historians in cataloguing their wealth of early buildings.

In Pickering Village, energetic and dedicated Ruby Fenton toured the village with us and showed us the fine slide collection which has been assembled by local enthusiasts of preservation. It includes a thorough study of the past history of the buildings in the area.

We want to thank the staff of the Ontario Archives who guided us over a two-year period in our search for original documents – land titles, assessment rolls, wills, newspapers, diaries, etc, etc. Their time is generously given to assist all visitors. In particular we want to thank Ken Macpherson, archivist, who discussed our project and helped us interpret complex material. Cathy Shepard assisted in our quest for various obscure details.

David Roberts, research co-ordinator, Heritage Administration Branch, Ministry of Culture and Recreation, discussed the results of his personal research with us and finally made a careful and knowledgeable reading of the manuscript.

This list would be incomplete without mention of Jan Kennedy, a dear friend and co-author with us of *Rural Roots*. To her go our thanks for her support and encouragement.

INDEX